P6-AGS-175

20TH CENTURY AMERICA

FOR BETTER

Immigration 1900-1910
Women's Worlds 1910-1920

Suzanne Perfect-Miller

DATE DUE

Brodart Co.   Cat. # 55 137 001   Printed in USA

3 9004 03209924 1

EDUCATION LIBRARY
DUNCAN McARTHUR HALL
QUEEN'S UNIVERSITY
KINGSTON, ONTARIO
K7L 3N6

20th CENTURY AMERICA

FOR BETTER

Immigration   1900–1910

Women's Worlds   1910–1920

Suzanne Perfect–Miller

SYNERGETICS

REACHING THROUGH TEACHING

© 1994 by Suzanne Perfect–Miller

For teacher use in a school, classroom quantities of student–pages may be duplicated. The reproduction of any part for an entire school, school system, or for commercial use is prohibited. Published by Synergetics,® P.O. Box 84, East WIndsor Hill, CT 06028.

ISBN   0–945984–71–5

Table of Contents

Introduction

Let's take a trip back to the beginning of this century. The world at this time was bubbling over with political unrest, unemployment, and famine and poverty. Thousands of people were deciding to embark on an unprecedented mass migration to the Land of Opportunity — America.

Imagine yourself as only one of these thousands. Life has been hard for you and your family. Jobs are scarce, and your family has struggled to survive. You have been told of the wonderful opportunities that will await you in America. Your relatives and friends have written that the streets are paved with gold. Just come on over! So you pack only the things that you can carry and embark on a journey that you hope will change your life for the better. The harrowing trip by steamship with its tight, airless quarters in steerage leaves you exhausted and sick. Strange people speak all different languages and frighten you a bit, and apprehension about your new home keeps you in tense anticipation of what will happen next.

The Ellis Island experience is even more difficult. You are worried that you might not be admitted into this new country. You see families broken up — some have red tags that mean admission, and others have blue tags. You dread to think what will happen to those who have blue tags pinned to their jackets. Will they get another chance? Will they be sent back? Finally, your family settles in New York City on the Lower East Side. What new experiences will you have? Will you adjust to all of this strangeness? Will you be able to go to school? What about the sweatshops you have heard about? What about new friends?

As immigrants began life in their new country with new challenges and hardships, so also were women experiencing struggles in an up–to–now man's world. For a long time women had been demanding equal rights and equal opportunities but were met with road blocks of values held to be traditional by the menfolk. Treated as second class citizens or worse, many women felt stifled. Many were held up as unrealistic goddesses on pedestals and could not offer opinions of import. No woman could vote, and few were allowed to drive the new cars. The primary duty of women was to home and family. Even the thought of holding a job was considered unfeminine and outrageous.

How could women change their lives? Would World War I have any affect on their position? Could they make a difference? Would they get the vote? What would you have done if you were living during these times? Would you have insisted on equality? Would you have joined the Suffragists in their march on Washington? Would you have joined the Navy in World War I? Would you agree with some women like Isabella Beecher Hooker (Harriet Beecher Stowe's suffragist sister) that women had a natural right to equality with men and a duty to exercise that right? How far would you be willing to go to fight for equal rights?

These are questions we will be confronting as, once again, we go back in time. As immigrants, we experience the difficulties of going through Ellis Island, and the hardships of living and working in our new country. We assume identities of our ancestors and, in costume, represent them. We stage a play about diverse peoples and how they live together. In "Women's Worlds," we learn of women's struggles as they go out into the work place and as they learn new trades to help in the war effort. We become Suffragists. We build a radio. We stage a "Chautauqua."

An excellent way to understand change as it happened to two diverse groups of people is to roleplay their lives—all described and illustrated in detail in the pages of this unique combination of two how–to handbooks in one:

20th Century America: For Better

"Immigration 1900–1910"

"Women's Worlds 1910–1920"

and

20th Century America: For Worse

"The Plunging Twenties"

"The Depressed Thirties"

For *20th Century America: For Worse*, please turn over the book. For *20th Century America: For Better*, please turn the page. . . .

Ways of Presenting Early 20th Century America, For Better, For Worse: Planning a 20th Century America Time Machine Program

This book gives instructions for creating an "Ellis Island Experience," fashioning costumes for immigrant children, constructing tenement buildings, staging a play, holding a "Suffragist Rally," building a metal auto racer, planning and performing in a Chautauqua, and putting together a radio. Students research their ancestors, present oral histories, and roleplay their ancestors.

These activities can be presented in several ways, depending on the objectives of the teacher, the abilities and interests of the children, and the school facilities. One simple method of organizing the *For Better* section is to divide the class into two groups: "Immigration" and "Women's Worlds." The two groups are assigned areas in the classroom in which to prepare and then present, for each other's benefit, their products and performances.

Another organizational method is used with two classes. One classroom becomes a group of immigrants and another classroom tackles the various positions and characters alluding to "Women's Worlds." For example, immigrants stage the "Ellis Island Experience" while the second group performs parts at a "Chautauqua."

My own preference is what I call "A 20th Century America Time Machine" in which groups from 1900–1920 combine with groups from 1920–1940. Parents, townspeople, and friends are invited to this school–wide program that takes place on the playground or gymnasium with the area being divided in 4 parts: "Immigration," "Women's Worlds," "The Plunging Twenties," and "The Depressed Thirties."

When the big day arrives—either an evening or Saturday—the invited guests discover what America was like in the early days of this century. A typical sequence of events can be found in the *For Worse* section of this book. "A 20th Century Time Machine" begins with the greeting to parents and friends by the Time Machine Captain. Guests travel back in time as they move from decade to decade, looking at exhibits from the "Tabletop Museum"; watching performances by immigrants at Ellis Island and in "Mrs. Dunn's Loverly, Loverly Farm"; enjoying the staging of a traditional Chautauqua with stock characters; viewing plantings and murals that are the result of government programs such as the WPA; and hearing music and song from the Jazz and Swing eras.

Background Information for the Teacher

Immigration: 1900–1910

In recent years newspapers and magazines have been filled with stories about the boat–people. Picked up miles out at sea in overcrowded and leaky boats and with few provisions, these people hope to escape poverty and political unrest in their home countries. Haitians follow the Windward Passage toward Cuba, often picking up others along the way. Haitians and Cubans voyage towards Miami. The lucky ones survive the sea and get to America. Others are picked up by the U.S. Coast Guard. Of those some are given political asylum, but most are returned to their homeland — to the same poverty and political persecution they tried so desperately to escape.

What of other immigrants? After the Vietnam War tens of thousands immigrated to this country from Vietnam, Cambodia, and Laos. They came to escape oppression and to find a better life. Mexicans seeking jobs routinely cross the U.S. border under cover of darkness, often finding work in the large cities and towns in America's Southwest. Chinese sign contracts with Chinese crime rings to gain entrance into this country. In doing so, they owe tens of thousands of dollars that they must pay off by working, often unlawfully. These people become indentured servants to modern "runners."

As the 20th century comes to a close it is time to take a look at America as it was at the beginning of this century. Then as now a flow of immigrants was coming to America. Between 1900 and 1910 almost nine million people came to the United States from Russia, Italy, the Far East, Turkey, Poland, and Albania. They came to find a better life because of religious persecution, political beliefs, or because they were just plain poor. Many truly believed the myth that America's streets were paved with gold. They came in teeming numbers on great steamships, formed long lines to be processed through Ellis and Angel Islands, and ended up in America's cities and farmlands. They worked in diverse jobs — in seafood canneries on the Gulf Coast, in the textile mills of the South, at spinning mills in Fall River, or the deep coal mines of Pennsylvania and West Virginia. Many of them settled in New York City and worked in sweatshops. "Runners," working for businessmen and boarding house owners, mingled among and enlisted newly arriving immigrants in order to get workers for the low–paying jobs and to find tenants to rent flats in the tenement buildings. Runners were paid by the head. As a result bosses got cheap labor, and tenement owners filled their buildings. While most people managed to stay and make a living in this new land, some did return to their homelands, driven back by poverty and discrimination. In one year — 1908 — 400,000 went back home.

The trip to America was rough and difficult. Steamships were overloaded, and most of the people traveled in steerage — packed down in the hold — with no running water or fresh air. When possible, everyone stayed up on deck. Food was cooked in large soup kettles, spooned into pails, and handed out to families. The typical fare averaged $12 per person, and immigrants arrived in New York disoriented, sick, and hungry.

Women's Worlds: 1910–1920

As 20th century America moved into its second decade, change occurred at an increasingly fast rate. At the turn of the century women were either placed on pedestals or were treated as second–class citizens. In their roles of homemakers, helpmates, and mothers they were not taken too seriously, could not vote, found it extremely difficult to do anything outside the home with the exception of volunteer work, and were even discouraged from driving cars (heaven forbid!). In 1901 author and critic Henry T. Finck (1881–1924) asked the question in an *Independent* article, "Should women be flowers or vegetables, ornamental or useful?" (See Bibliography.) He went on to announce that it was not only selfish, but suicidal, for young middle and upper class woman to work because (a) they took jobs away from poor men and women and (b) by working they would ruin their chances for marriage and, thus, die as old maids or—worse—as "new women" as suffragists called themselves. He spoke of "physical morality," which was nervous collapse in women who strived to compete with men in the work force.

Regardless of Finck's outlook (and many others') family traditions and home life were changing. While married women still had the prime responsibility to their families, single women sought independence, began working and earned money, and demanded equality. By 1910 these emancipated working girls numbered over seven million. With their bobbed hair, loose clothing, and growing self–reliance they raised their voices and their numbers increased.

American suffragists met with their English counterparts and came home strengthened in their beliefs and ready to adopt militant tactics. The women's rights movement had been strong in Europe since the mid–1800's. Women were imprisoned when they went on hunger strikes to achieve their goals. In prison the guards often beat them, put them in solitary confinement, and brutally force–fed them, all because of their beliefs.

In 1910 after years of fairly quiet revolution women took to the streets to march for their right to vote. During the next few years marchers doubled, then quadrupled, and by 1915 had swelled to 40,000 in one New York City parade. Militant women, such as Lucretia Mott and Alice Paul, held teas and rallies that drew crowds of sympathetic men and women. Women began to win the vote one state at a time (by 1909—Idaho, Wyoming, Utah, Colorado; by 1911—California, Washington; by 1916—Oregon, Nevada, Arizona, Kansas, Illinois).

Many men and women resisted the movement. Anti–suffrage songs such as "Mind the Baby, I Must Vote To–Day" and "Be Good to California, Mr. Wilson (California Was Good To You)" were popular. This latter song referred to the fact that the Women's Party hoped that Californian women would vote against the anti–suffrage Wilson. It didn't work; California women were more interested in peace than in suffrage issues. Finally in June, 1919, Congress passed the 19th Amendment to the Constitution that stated that "no citizen could be denied the right to vote on account of sex."

As the students complete the activities in this curriculum unit, they picture themselves among the immigrants coming to this new land by reading about fictional immigrant children. They may imagine themselves as Krysia or Zanya from Poland (*An Ellis Island Christmas*), 10–year old Edward or his brother Guiseppe from Italy (*Immigrant Kids*), the little Irish girl, Bria, (*Cobblestone, Dec. 1982*), or George from Czechoslovakia, (*Album of the Great Wave of Immigration*). Other stories could be used instead. In addition, several stories are suggested along with many of the activities. The teacher can use these as reading lessons either by requiring the students to read them or by reading them to the students. In this way the students will gain an increasingly precise idea of what life was like during the first decades of the twentieth century while they enjoy good historical fiction. Students can also read the stories and develop characters to be roleplayed at "A 20th Century America Time Machine."

It is important also that the students see lots of photographs and film or video excerpts that introduce the life of the first decades of the twentieth century. The teacher should be prepared to show these films to depict life in the tenements of New York City, life during the Great Depression, and to show the dress and mannerisms of the eras. Several suggestions are listed in the Bibliography. Many more are available.

The first lesson in the *For Worse* section of the book is introductory for all the decades. It asks the teacher to show film or video excerpts from movies that show life in those decades, a practice that is continued throughout the unit. The students need to use some sort of graphic organizer for the notes they take from these films. One is suggested following the lesson, which can be varied to meet the needs and ages of the students.

20ᵀᴴ CENTURY AMERICA

FOR BETTER

Immigration   1900-1910

Lesson Plan 1

What's In A Name?

OBJECTIVE: To find out the origin and meaning of our family names.

MATERIALS: References (See *Cobblestone* magazine, 1983; Lila Perl's *The Great Ancestor Hunt*; and Ennis Duling's *What's in an American Name?*); world map; "What's in a Name?"*
*Provided at the end of the lesson.

LENGTH OF TIME: 30 minutes in class (introduction of lesson and discussion after completion of activity at home); 15–30 minutes at home.

SPECIAL INSTRUCTIONS: If the teacher is concerned for any reason about students researching their family backgrounds, the students can research any name that intrigues them using reference books. If the people are living, letters could be written to them in some cases.

PROCEDURE:

1. The teacher ask students what their names tells them and accepts all stories and answers.

2. The teacher then explains that last names often indicate from what country a person's ancestors emigrated. Although some of our ancestors may have Americanized their names, which might have been too long or too difficult to pronounce, the shortened versions still supply us with information about where they might have originated. For example, the German surname, *Morganstern*, means Morningstar in English; the German surname, *Mueller*, means Miller in English; the Italian surname, *Verdi*, means Green in English; and the Dutch surname, *Krommezee*, means Gramercy (an archaic word for Thanks) in English.

2. The teacher asks the students if any of them have surnames that they think may have come from another country. These names are listed on the board with their possible country of origin.

3. Students are given the checklist, "What's in a Name?" They take it home to complete with the help of their parents or grandparents.

4. When the information on students' last names has been collected, the teacher asks the class questions like the following:

   a. How many different countries are represented in our classroom?

   b. Where are these countries located on the world map?

   c. Did anyone learn any other interesting piece of information about their family name that they are willing to share?

d. Did anyone learn that their surname had been changed or shortened or why this change occurred?

5. The teacher has the students research the meaning of their surnames in any available references. (See list under "Materials" section.)

What's In a Name?

Last Name_____

What country does your name come from?_____

Does your name have a special meaning?_____

Was your name changed?_____

Do you know why?_____

If your name was changed, what was the original family name?_____

Lesson Plan 2

An Ancestor Comes To Life

OBJECTIVES:
To interview family members and record the information, the feelings, and other observations (oral history).

To select one ancestor to roleplay in "Activity 4: An Ellis Island Experience."

MATERIALS:
Reference books such as *Immigrant Kids* (Russell Freedman, 1980), *The Family Storytelling Handbook* (Anne Pellowski, 1987), *My Family Tree Workbook* (Rosemary Chorzempa, 1989), and *Roots for Kids* (Susan P. Beller, 1989); notebook, tape recorder, or camcorder.

SPECIAL INSTRUCTIONS:
Since most of this lesson is completed at home, the teacher needs only to help the students to know the kinds of things for which they will be searching. Younger students can record the information on sheets similar to those in *My Family Tree Workbook*. Time (as much as 3 or 4 weeks) may be needed for the students to complete this assignment at home.

If the teacher has individual students whose families came to this country long before the memory of any living relative, the student might be allowed to research the background of a famous individual. It is also possible to put the student in touch with the genealogical library of the Church of Latter Day Saints. More than 700 branch libraries are located throughout the United States, Canada, and other countries. These free libraries maintain microfilm collections of more than 88 million persons, most from before 1900. Some of the electronic services like Prodigy® also have genealogical bulletin boards.

Other problems arise with recent immigrants, those who do not know their parents, Native Americans, or other students. The teacher must be flexible. Above all no child should be embarrassed in any way. Everyone should be given the option of researching a famous personality who came to this country in the early 1900's or even someone unknown to the student. For example, the student might look for information in a genealogical library about someone with a surname the same as theirs, their adoptive parents, or even a neighbor or friend of the family. The book by C.A. Bales or some of the fictional titles listed in the Bibliography can help children decide on a character if a family member is unavailable.

LENGTH OF TIME:
At least one hour at home (more if possible); about 30 minutes in class to introduce the activity; several 15–30 minute sessions where class shares information and experiences.

PROCEDURE:

1. The teacher asks the students if their family has passed on stories to them about their

family or family members. For example, the family may have told stories about life when they were the same age as the students. The teacher lets the students share some of these stories and asks the students if they wouldn't like to find out more about their families.

2. The class brainstorms a list of what they would like to know about their ancestors. This list is written on the blackboard and may include questions like the following:

    a. When did our ancestors come to America?

    b. What did they do for a living in the country from which they came?

    c. What brought them to this country?

    d. How old were they when they came?

    e. Where did they live when they first got here? Why did they live in that place?

    f. What did they do for fun when they were children?

    g. What stories about their family have been passed down?

2. The teacher asks the class how they could learn the answers to their questions. A list of possible places and people to ask is brainstormed and put on the blackboard. The reference books can be consulted to learn of additional places.

3. The teacher explains that, since their lists include parents, grandparents, and other members of the family as sources, they should interview them. They will need to write down their major questions but can write or tape their answers.

4. The teacher reminds the students to ask about and record any family stories that have been passed down through generations. These stories might be funny, sad, or amazing stories.

5. The students should also get family photographs if possible. They duplicate quite well on a good copy machine if they are unframed and can then be included in the student's notebook with the rest of the family history. Older students might videotape the photographs, other family artifacts, or the storytelling of a family member.

6. If possible, each student chooses a specific family character to be developed from his or her family history to roleplay in the "Ellis Island Experience." If no member of the family seems appropriate for whatever reason, the student can select an imaginary person, well–known immigrant from the time period, or even a composite person. Once settled upon, however, the student should stay with the characterization. For example, a young man of 18 who was raised on a farm or a mother with four small children. The teacher records this information for each student.

7. The students each find out as much additional information as possible about the character they select. This information needs to include such things as:

    a. Full name of person

    b. Nationality

    c. Age at time of immigration or when he or she lived in America

    d.   Appearance from photographs or from descriptions

    e.   Language spoken before coming to America

    f.   Occupation if the person came as an adult

    g.   Number and names of brothers and sisters; names of parents

    h.   What responsibilities and duties the person had if a child

    i.   What the person did for fun if a child

8. The teacher encourages the students to write to family members who live farther away. Several weeks may be needed for return of the information.

9. The teacher can have sharing sessions with the students at several times during the next few weeks where students share their material and report their successes and failures in recording their oral history.

10. The students can record their information on a page patterned after that in any one of the suggested books.

1900 - 1910

Lesson Plan 3
Costumes for Characterizations

OBJECTIVES: To develop an actual character from your family background using information obtained through family records, photos, and interviews.

To costume the character for "An Ellis Island Experience."

MATERIALS: *Immigrant Kids* (Russell Freedman, 1980); Illustrations: "New Arrivals,"* "Men and Women–Early 1900's;"* "Boys and Girls–Early 1900's,"* "Costumes for Boys and Girls;"* *Clues to American Dress*, (Hartley, 1992); information from family records from Lesson 2, including any pictures.

*Provided at the end of the lesson.

SPECIAL INSTRUCTIONS: In making plans for recreating the "Ellis Island Experience," the teacher sets aside an hour on a Friday afternoon or at another convenient time for students to dress up and practice introductions.

The precautionary measures noted under "Special Instructions" for Lesson 4 apply here as well.

LENGTH OF TIME: 30 minutes for research and brainstorming; 1 hour at school for dressing up and practicing; time at home for gathering costume materials.

PROCEDURE:

1. The teacher asks students to name differences in clothing they find in family photographs compared to what they or their parents wear today. These differences are listed on the blackboard. The teacher explains that, if they are going to roleplay these family members, they will need to have costumes that are similar to the kind of clothing their ancestors wore at that time.

2. The teacher gives the illustrations to the students and discusses possibilities for costuming. The teacher also shows photos from Freedman's *Immigrant Kids* to illustrate the type of clothing worn in the early 1900's.

3. The students brainstorm characteristics of the clothing that people wore around 1900 and discuss what they have at home that might be used in creating a costume. They choose dark colors or small prints for dresses. Boys may push up pantlegs on dark–colored trousers to simulate knickers or short pants. Both boys and girls wear tights (black for boys; black or white for girls).

4. The students collect articles of clothing to bring to school for the costumes.

5. At school students mix and match articles with one another. The teacher can also have a Friday Dress–up afternoon where the students help each other out and dress in the costumes they have created.

6. The students dress in costume and practice introducing themselves to one another. It is important to stay in character.

BOYS AND GIRLS · EARLY 1900's

FOR BOYS

COSTUMES

KNICKERS + TIGHTS
SUSPENDERS (OPTIONAL)
WHITE SHIRT, JACKET (OPTIONAL)
HIGH TOPS

WESTERN UNION

HATS
&
CAPS *

* NO BASEBALL CAPS

FOR GIRLS

DRESS - PLAIN OR SMALL PRINT
PINAFORE (OPTIONAL)
HAIR RIBBONS AND BOWS

KERCHIEF
SHAWL
(OPTIONAL)

TIGHTS (BLACK OR WHITE)
BOOTS OR SHOES (PLAIN)

Lesson Plan 4
An Ellis Island Experience

OBJECTIVE: To roleplay a scene at Ellis Island at the turn of the century using a chosen character.

MATERIALS: Identity tags and pins (doctor, interpreter, registration clerk); red tags; blue tags; quarantine pins; *An Ellis Island Christmas* (Leighton, 1992); role cards;* chalk; fact sheet, "An Ellis Island Experience."
*Provided at the end of the lesson.

SPECIAL INSTRUCTIONS: The teacher assigns two students to be doctors and gives each a piece of chalk. At least one other student is assigned to be an interpreter and another the registration clerk. Large classes will need two registration clerks and several interpreters. If any students in the class (or school) have come to the U.S. as immigrants, they might be willing to talk to the class about what immigration is like today. Be sure that any student who volunteers feels comfortable about doing so. ESL (English as a Second Language) classes might be a source for such a speaker. Teachers may know an adult who entered the U.S. as an immigrant who would be willing to speak to the class.

LENGTH OF TIME: 1 hour or more.

PROCEDURE:

1. The teacher tells the students that the imigrants experienced many different emotions when they first arrived. It is a little like what would happen if the students went to a mall in a strange city in a foreign country. In order to find their way around or buy anything, the students would have to strike up conversations with strangers who spoke a different language. How would this situation make them feel? How would other people react to them? What emotions would they be likely to experience?

2. The teacher reads Maxinne Rhea Leighton's *An Ellis Island Christmas* to the class. This marvelous story captures the courage, uncertainty, and wonder of a young Polish girl as she experiences Ellis Island. As the story is read aloud, the teacher stops at appropriate places and asks the students to predict what will happen next.

3. The teacher distributes the fact sheet, "An Ellis Island Experience," and the students read it. Questions like the following are asked:

   a. Why would the U.S. have had the immigrants enter the country through Ellis Island in the early 1900's?

   b. Why do you think that Ellis Island got the nickname of Heartbreak Island?

   c. What might it have been like to enter the U.S. for the first time?

   d. Why were the doctors so impersonal and unfriendly?

4. The teacher assigns students to the following roles: two doctors, one or two registration clerks, one or more interpreters. Each player is given a roleplay card.

5. Students will definitely have strong feelings about "An Ellis Island Experience." The teacher can lead a class discussion by asking questions like the following:

    a. How did the experience of going through the Ellis Island processing center before being allowed into the United States make you feel?

    b. Was it fair? Why or why not?

    c. If you were not allowed into the U.S. in the roleplaying we just did, how did you feel?

    d. Did the way you felt depend upon the reasons for your denial of admission?

    e. What will you plan to do if you are sent back to your old country?

    f. What will those of you who were allowed into the U.S. do? How will you decide where to live?

    g. What did you learn from this roleplaying exercise?

    h. What did you like or dislike about the roleplaying?

6. If possible, the teacher invites a student or adult who has come to this country as an immigrant to talk to the class and express their feelings.

Role Cards

Doctor #1

As the Doctor you stand at the head of the line, examining each immigrant by sight. You may mark "L" for lameness, "H" for heart, or "FT" for foot problems. Mark the letter with chalk on the immigrant's clothing at the shoulder. After you finish marking the immigrant, ask those whom you have marked to return to their seats. Remember, one person in six failed to gain entry into this country because of mental or physical problems. Do not exceed this number as Doctor #2 will also be checking the immigrants.

Doctor #2

You examine the patients who have not been asked to sit down. Peer into the eyes of each person to look for trachoma, a highly contagious eye disease that was the primary reason people couldn't get admitted into this country. Chalk an "E" on any sufferers of trachoma.

Interpreter

Attach the card that says "Interpreter" to your shoulder. Write the language you speak on your card. Some Interpreters may speak more than one language. Examples are Italian, French, Greek, Armenian, Czech, or Russian. Immigrants who wish to communicate with the Registration Clerk or the Doctors must find an Interpreter who speaks their language. Often no interpreter was available.

Registration Clerk

As Registration Clerk you sit at a desk and ask the following questions of each immigrant who has passed the medical screening:

1. What is your name and nationality?
2. What is your occupation?
3. Can you read and write?
4. Have you ever been in prison?
5. Do you have any money?
6. Where do you plan to live?
7. Do you believe in polygamy (marrying more than one person)?
8. Do you plan to overthrow the government?

Depending on the answers to the questions, you hand out a red tag (admitting the person) or a blue tag (rejecting the person).

An Ellis Island Experience

Imagine yourself as an immigrant entering a strange new world. How would you feel? You've traveled for weeks on a ship packed full of people speaking many languages. Probably you spent many days feeling sick. Certainly you are apprehensive and anxious. Maybe you are meeting your father or other relatives who had come before you. They have already prepared a new home for you. Some of you aren't meeting anyone at all. You are here with your family to start a new life. Some of the children on the boat with you have traveled all by themselves. Until 1908, children could be sent all alone. After that year laws stipulated that they must travel with an adult.

When your ship steamed into New York Harbor, the first sight you saw was the Statue of Liberty, welcoming you to America. You dock at a pier on the Hudson River and identity tags are pinned to your clothing. Everyone must get into ferryboats that carry you over to Ellis Island. You hear some immigrants murmuring that it's called Heartbreak Island: and you don't know why. How do you think it got that nickname?

Officials shout and jostle you along. What a huge room! It's the inspection hall where you will all be examined. Two doctors stand at the end of the lines. They are from the U.S. Health Service, and they're looking for any physical or mental problems among the immigrants. You notice that an old man has a large "H" chalked on his shoulder. The doctor draws an "L" on the shoulder of a little girl. Both these people leave the line. Getting by the second doctor is unnerving. He stands right in front of the crowd. As you approach, he grabs your eyelid with a cold metal buttonhook and looks intently into your eye. What is going on? This is all so confusing.

Slowly you move on to the registration desk where an interpreter asks you a lot of questions. You answer them very carefully. They hand you a red tag, which means you are allowed to enter the United States of America.

Lesson Plan 5
Building Tenements

OBJECTIVES: To build tenement buildings for the creative dramatic piece "Mrs. Dunn's Loverly, Loverly Farm" or for "A 20th Century America Time Machine."

To study building facades from the turn of the century and paint facsimiles of these facades.

MATERIALS: Fact sheet, "Life in America";* Tenement Building, Lower East Side Illustration;* cardboard refrigerator boxes (1 box per tenement block); yardsticks; black paint and assorted brushes; scissors or X–Acto knives; *Immigrant Kids* (Russell Freedman, 1980), *Coal Mine Peaches* (Michelle Dionette, 1991) or other books listed in the Bibliography for pictures; resource books and encyclopedias showing architectural styles of the 19th century.

*Provided at the end of the lesson.

SPECIAL INSTRUCTIONS: Short fictional stories, like many of those listed in the Bibliography, help students develop a concept of where people might have lived. Stories can be read by the students at home, during silent reading time in language arts or other classes, or the teacher or a student can read to the class. For this lesson the teacher can select one that talks about the tenement buildings in which many people lived.

The teacher needs to look through resource books and encyclopedias to locate several pictures showing typical homes of immigrants in the 1900's in places like New York City.

LENGTH OF TIME: Approximately 2 hours.

PROCEDURE :

1. The teacher shows pictures of tenement buildings on the Lower East Side of New York City and asks the students to describe them. They can list similarities and differences from their homes.

2. The teacher distributes the fact sheet, "Life in America," and the students read it. In order to assess students' understanding of life in America at the turn of the century, the teacher can ask questions like the following:

   a. Name some of the things about life in America at the turn of the century that you would have liked.

   b. Name some of the things you would have disliked about that life.

   c. Why did many people from the same country tend to live together near each other?

   d. Why did most of the children work instead of going to school? What happened to the money that they earned?

e. Why were the immigrants usually unable to get better jobs?

f. How would an immigrant's life differ today? How would it be similiar?

3. The teacher explains that the class will construct several tenement buildings. For each tenement block that the students make they complete the instructions that follow:

a. Open and lay flat a refrigerator box.

b. Cut off flaps from boxes. These may be reserved for making chimneys or other architectural features such as columns or fire escapes. (A)

c. Using yardsticks, pencil down each fold on the box to make 4 separate buildings. Divide each building into three, four, or five stories. Pencil in the divisions. To make an awning for a first–floor store pencil in lines and cut along two sides and the bottom, as shown. (B) Fold up the cut awning.

d. Pencil in windows, porches, fire escapes, shop windows and doors. (C)

e. Paint over penciled lines for a more dramatic effect.

f. Make a double tenement with two singles or any combination you wish. (D). Glue or staple on chimneys.

g. Staple to bulletin boards; attach to artists' easels for free–standing buildings.

h. Finish off the effect by hanging washlines with clothing between the buildings. (C & D)

i. If you wish to paint these buildings, use red or yellow for brick or brown for wood. You must paint both the front and the back of the refrigerator box. If only the front is painted, much warping will occur. Simply painting black lines will not warp the buildings.

LOWER EAST SIDE

TENEMENT BUILDING

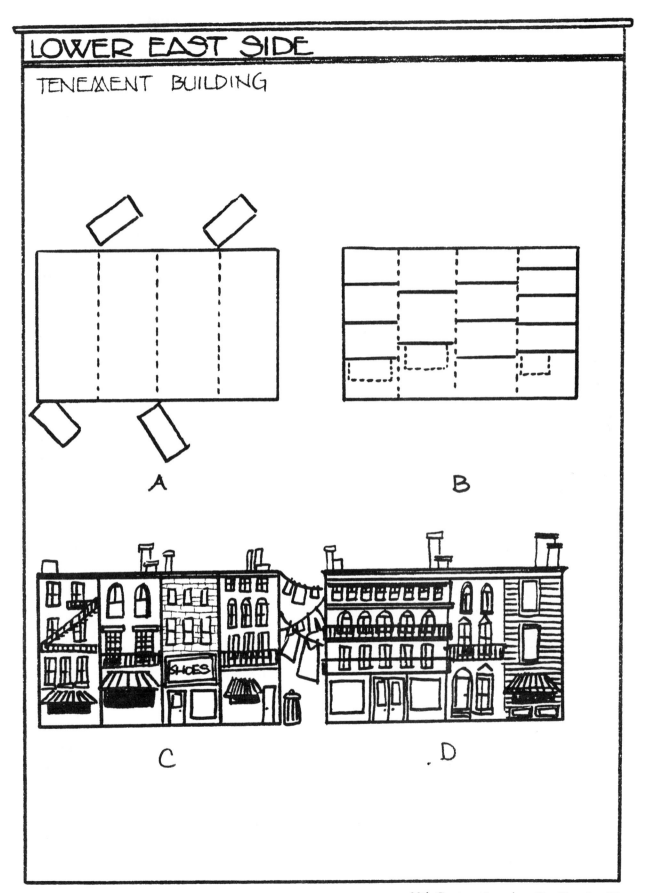

A

B

C

D

Life in America

Many immigrant families lived on the Lower East Side of New York City. If they were lucky and escaped the unscrupulous runners who met immigrants coming into the city, they found that apartments were numerous and could be rented reasonably. If the family could afford it, it had the luxury of a three–room apartment and maybe even running water. In most tenements, however, water faucets were found in the halls, and water had to be hauled to the apartment.

Life in a tenement building was difficult. Tenements were often crowded as many people took in boarders to help with the rent. As a result many people slept on straw pallets placed around the main room, which also served as kitchen and living room. Crowding usually meant that children shared their straw pallet with their brothers and sisters. Most apartments meant climbing stairs, frequently 5 or 6 flights. Usually a store like a shoe store or a fish market was on the first floor of the tenement building. Apartments were cold in the winter months and so oppressively hot during the summer that everyone sat outside on stoops, ran up onto the roof, or fled to fire escapes. Lots of times children would camp on the fire escapes by rigging up tents and sleeping outside.

Everyone in the family usually worked at home or outside the home. Plenty of jobs were available, but ones that paid well were hard to find. Both girls and boys worked long hours in various jobs. Many worked at home helping their family sew clothing, make cloth flowers, or roll cigars. Others worked 10 hours a day, often 7 days a week, in one of the many sweatshops that sprang up all over the city. Sweatshops were workshops that were hot and confining where people worked long hours for very low pay. Though the law stipulated that children under 14 years old must be in school, it was frequently not enforced. Children often lied about their age in order to help out their families. Some factories even illegally reserved a special spot for the youngest children who did easy work, like trimming excess threads off clothing. Shop foremen hid these children when an inspector came around.

By the age of 10 or 12 most immigrant children had started work in factories, stores, or mills where they did the job of an adult, but earned about two dollars a week. Other children ran errands, became bootblacks, or peddled newspapers. Newsies, as newspaper boys were called, might even live on their own. Either homeless or because there were too many mouths to feed at home, these boys took to the streets. They lived by their wits, bought newspapers for a set price and sold them for a few pennies more, and stayed in lodging houses run by the Children's Aid Society. For six cents a night they had a clean bed; for an additional 12 cents they received two meals a day. These children were called street arabs. They had their own set of rules and code of honor and answered to nicknames like "Cheater," "Joker," and "The Snitch." Those children who were fortunate enough to attend school worked at various jobs on afternoons and weekends.

Children who had some time to play took to the streets or sidewalks, which were filled with exciting things to see and do. Boys played baseball and stickball; girls played Potsy (hopscotch) and simple games like Catch and Juggle. In these games they used beanbags made by filling cloth bags with cherry pits. Instead of dolls, which were rare, girls often cared for and played with their baby sisters and brothers. Both boys and girls loved the organ grinder with his hurdy–gurdy and his performing monkey. Children from all over the world quickly learned English by mingling with each other and trying to communicate.

LOWER EAST SIDE   1900

CREATIVE DRAMA

Lesson Plan 6
Creative Drama: "Mrs. Dunn's Loverly, Loverly Farm"

OBJECTIVES: To produce a creative dramatic piece about people from different cultures living together in a tenement during the early 20th century.

To create different characterizations from the story.

To appreciate different cultures and to see how they blend.

MATERIALS: *The Witch of Fourth Street & Other Stories* (Myron Levoy, 1972); Synopsis of "Mrs. Dunn's Loverly, Loverly Farm";* tenement building (Lesson Plan 5); step ladder; props (Lesson Plan 7); watering can.

*Provided at the end of the lesson.

SPECIAL INSTRUCTIONS: If for any reason the teacher is unable to obtain the book, *The Witch of Fourth Street & Other Stories*, the synopsis can be used instead. The class will benefit from reading as many of the stories in this book as possible. The characters in the various stories cover a variety of lifestyles. The props for the dramatic piece are constructed in Lesson Plan 7.

LENGTH OF TIME: Two 45–minute periods.

PROCEDURE:

1. The teacher reads "Mrs. Dunn's Loverly, Loverly Farm" to the class. Several characters are mentioned in this story that are expanded upon in the other stories in *The Witch of Fourth Street*. The teacher can have various students read these other stories so that they are familiar with them in more detail. The students characterize what it was like to live in a tenement.

2. The teacher asks the class questions like the following:

    a. How many nationalities were represented in the story?

    b. In what ways did the neighbors work together?

    c. Which was your favorite immigrant character? Why?

    d. What problems did the neighbors experience?

3. The teacher lists the characters on the board as the students name them. The class discusses each characterization by listing something about each one. The students will develop a list similar to the following:

- Mrs. Dunn—Irish, loves gardens;
- Mr. Dunn—Irish, hauls coal, makes garden boxes for Mrs. Dunn;
- Cathy—Daughter of the Dunns; (Students can read "The Witch of Fourth Street" for more information.")

- Neil — Son of the Dunns;
- Aaron Kandel — Ukranian, brings matzo for chickens, Class A roller–skater; (Students can read "Aaron's Gift" in the same book.)
- Fred Reinhardt — Brings scraps of pumpernickel for chickens;
- Vincent DeMarco — Italian, brings chick peas for chickens, 11 years old; (Students can read "Vincent–the–Good" and the "Electric Train.")
- Mrs. Callahan — Irish, lives on first floor, wants to cook;
- Noreen — Mrs. Callahan's daughter; (Students can read "The Fish Angel.")
- Mrs. Grotowski — Lives on second floor, wants apartment painted;
- Mrs. Cherney — Lives on fourth floor;
- Mr. Warfield — The terrible, horrible landlord;
- Amelia — Chicken #1, Rhode Island Red, proud, struts around;
- Agatha — Chicken #2, busybody;
- Adelene — Chicken #3, shy, preens; and
- Narrator.

4. Students choose the parts that they would like to play. The teacher helps them discuss how each character might be played and mime facial expressions, body movements, and walks. Questions like the following are asked:

- How might the landlord look? How might he walk?
- What does a shy chicken look like? A busybody chicken?
- Mrs. Callahan needs her stove fixed. She likes to cook. Mime Mrs. Callahan stirring up a bowl of Irish soda bread.
- Mrs. Grotowski has dreams. Mime a dreamy Mrs. Grotowski.
- Mime Aaron roller skating.
- What does "Vincent–the–Good" look like?

5. The class reads the synopsis of the story (if they have not read the story or to refresh their memories) and writes an outline of the plot. They include stage directions as the scenario develops. First, the students tell the story to each other. Then while they stay in character they add dialogue to the story.

6. The characters climb the step ladder to sit in designated spots.

- Mrs. Callahan sits on the floor (first floor) miming mixing bread.
- Mrs. Grotowski sits on the first step (second floor) looking dreamy.
- Mrs. Dunn sits on second step (third floor) watering plants.
- Mrs. Cherney sits on third step (fourth floor) hand–sewing, perhaps.

7. The narrator introduces the story and fills in the plot as the story unfolds.

8. As Mrs. Dunn buys the chickens, they strut and preen around the front of the stepladder. Chicken–characters can write a short chant or poem to be spoken in unison.

9. When Mr. Warfield arrives and gets water on his head there is a great deal of yelling up and down the stepladder.

10. Before the practice is completed, the class makes props, which get moved up and down the stepladder and ultimately attached to the roof. See Lesson Plan 7.

11. The students expand their list of ideas about life in a tenement house. Where possible, the students incorporate these additional ideas into their dramatization.

12. The actors practice with 3 or 4 run–throughs and tighten the interpretation of the dramatic piece for performing at "A 20th Century Time Machine."

Synopsis
"Mrs. Dunn's Loverly, Loverly Farm"

Mrs. Dunn has been promised that when the family comes to this country from Ireland she will have her farm. They move into a tenement near Second Avenue in New York City and meet their neighbors who have come here from all over the world. Mr. Dunn finds a job delivering coal. She and Mr. Dunn save their pennies for their dream farm, but after one year they still have less than $15 between them.

Mrs. Dunn decides that, unless she starts her farm NOW, they'll never have one. She buys a hen and Mr. Dunn builds a coop. Two more hens arrive, and he fashions nests out of old felt hats. Soon the hens are laying eggs. Children living in the building bring various bits of foods to the hens, and Mrs. Dunn sometimes gives them eggs in exchange.

Soon Mrs. Dunn plants vegetables. Mr. Dunn builds big boxes and fills them with dirt. They plant tomatoes, beans, onions, potatoes and lots of herbs. The boxes are placed on the fire escape to get the sun. In very little time lush growing plants are inside and outside the apartment. They are tended carefully by the whole family. One day Mrs. Dunn is watering her fire escape garden when Mr. Warfield, the landlord, comes to collect the rents. Mrs. Dunn accidently pours water right on Mr. Warfield's head. He looks up and becomes outraged at what he thinks are trees growing on the fire escape.

Racing into the building, he is first stopped by Mrs. Callahan who has already sent her daughter, Noreen, to warn the Dunns. She holds him off by loudly complaining that he has to fix her no–good stove. Finally, escaping her, he gets to the second floor, only to be accosted by Mrs. Grotowski who tells him about her dream in which she tears up her rent money and cooks it. She has been waiting patiently to have her apartment painted. More altercations occur until Mr. Warfield escapes to the third floor and pounds on Mrs. Dunn's door.

Meanwhile, neighbors have been racing to hide the evidence. Chickens go to Mrs. DeMarco and Mrs. Kandel. (The third chicken flies onto Mrs. Dunn's chandelier.) Boxes are plucked off the fire escape and hidden under beds in apartments above and below.

Mr. Warfield wants to know what's going on. He rushes in and discovers all kinds of vegetation growing here and there. But Mrs. Dunn outfoxes and outtalks Mr. Warfield by suggesting that he would be so kind to allow her to use the roof for her farm. He sputters and squawks (the chickens do, too) and realizes that the neighbors would look kindly on him if this is allowed. He concedes and races away with a chicken clinging to his hat.

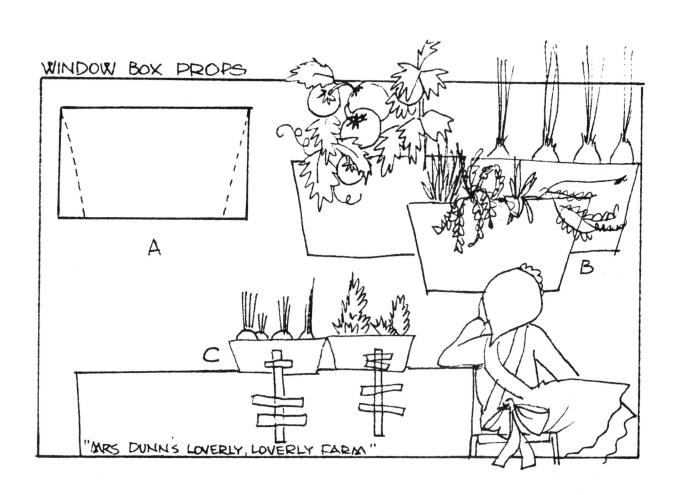

WINDOW BOX PROPS

A

B

C

"MRS DUNN'S LOVERLY, LOVERLY FARM"

Lesson Plan 7

Cardboard Props for "Mrs. Dunn's Loverly, Loverly Farm"

OBJECTIVE: To plan and make props for the creative dramatic piece.

MATERIALS: 7 heavy box–cardboard pieces cut to 12" x 18"; colored construction paper; scissors; crayons or felt tip markers; (optional) rulers or dowels; planning process sheet, "Planning the Props for Mrs. Dunn."*
*Provided at the end of the lesson.

SPECIAL INSTRUCTIONS: Before this lesson occurs, the teacher and students gather garden catalogs from home. They find out which vegetables and herbs could grow in the New York City area. The students list the herbs that Mrs. Dunn might have planted. They carefully observe the leaves and way the plants grow so that their props will be more authentic. The students can use garden row markers to make their garden look more like the real thing.

LENGTH OF TIME: 45 minutes.

PROCEDURE:

1. The teacher asks the students to identify any props they need to make for the creative dramatic piece, "Mrs. Dunn's Lovery, Lovery Farm." The students are divided into pairs, and each pair completes the planning process sheet, "Planning Props for Mrs. Dunn." Students should name such things as window boxes, vegetable plants, flowers, and felt–hat chicken coops.

2. The students look at home for felt hats that they can use or for a substitute.

3. The students make various vegetables by following the instructions:

   a. Cut sides of each 12" x 18" cardboard piece for window box, as shown. (A)

   b. Make large green foliage for each of 6 window boxes: tomatoes, string beans, potatoes, onions, and various herbs and spices. (B)

   c. Glue foliage on and over the sides of each box.

   d. (Optional) Attach rulers or dowels to the backs of each vegetable piece for easy holding, especially if it will be handed up and down while sitting on the the step ladder. Windowboxes can be more easily taped to the rooftop at the end of the story by taping the rulers to the boxes. (C) (A student can be stationed behind the tenement building to fasten the tape on the boxes.)

Planning the Props for Mrs. Dunn

1. List the props that would make the roleplaying of Mrs. Dunn's garden more realistic. Draw sketches to help you understand your objective.

2. What materials would you need for each one of the props? List them and where you can find each one.

3. What problems might you encounter in making these props?

4. Share the plan with the class. Have you forgotten anything? Can suggestions be made to improve the ideas. Can any problems you anticipate be solved?

20ᵗʰ CENTURY AMERICA
FOR BETTER

Women's Worlds 1910-1920

Lesson Plan 8
Women's Suffrage Rally

OBJECTIVES: To participate in a rally in which participants take both sides of the issue.
To prepare a program for the rally.

MATERIALS: Fact sheet, "Women's Suffrage—Pro and Con;"* "Famous Suffragists List";* "Reasons Women Should Vote List";* art materials for posters, yardsticks, masking tape; video of a political rally (optional); Biography Cubes.*
*Provided at the end of the lesson.

SPECIAL INSTRUCTIONS: The teacher can make a videotape from a news program that shows a political rally to show the students what goes on at a rally.

LENGTH OF TIME: One hour or more if desired.

PROCEDURE:

1. The teacher asks the students if any of them have ever been to a football or other sports rally. What are pep rallies supposed to do for the teams? Are there any other groups that have rallies? (political rallies; religious rallies) A video of a political or other rally can be shown.

2. The teacher explains to the class that they will be holding a rally about women's suffrage. Women were not allowed to vote in the U. S. until the ratification of the 19th amendment to the Constitution on August 26, 1920. During the second decade of this century and for years before that time, however, many women were active in the suffragist movement.

3. The names on the "Famous Suffragists List" are divided by the teacher among the students in the class. Students locate five facts about each suffragist they are assigned and place the information on a Biography Cube. The cubes are glued together and hung from the ceiling so that all the students can share the information.

4. The teacher distributes copies of the fact sheet, "Women's Suffrage—Pro and Con" and "Reasons Women Should Vote List." The class is divided into groups of 3–5 students who have 15–20 minutes to develop their arguments on each issue.

5. The teacher randomly divides the class in half. One half is assigned the pro position on women's suffrage; the other half is assigned the con position.

6. Students who are on the pro side may take part in the rally as one of the characters they researched.

7. The students on each side of the issue prepare short speeches and posters to promote

their side of the argument. The posters are taped to yardsticks to use in marches.

8. The rally is held with each side speaking out on their beliefs. A parade or march can be held through the school with each side holding their posters. If students wish to do so, songs or other material may be prepared to enliven the rally. The speeches are given. The speeches and rally can also be held as a presentation for another class or grade. It can be presented at "A 20th Century America Time Machine."

9. At the conclusion of the rally the class holds a discussion centering around questions like the following:

    a.   Were any of the points made by either side discrimnatory?

    b.   What points that were made are reasonable? To whom are they reasonable?

    c.   What additional issues should be addressed that were omitted by either side?

Biography Cube

Enlarge and add tabs for gluing

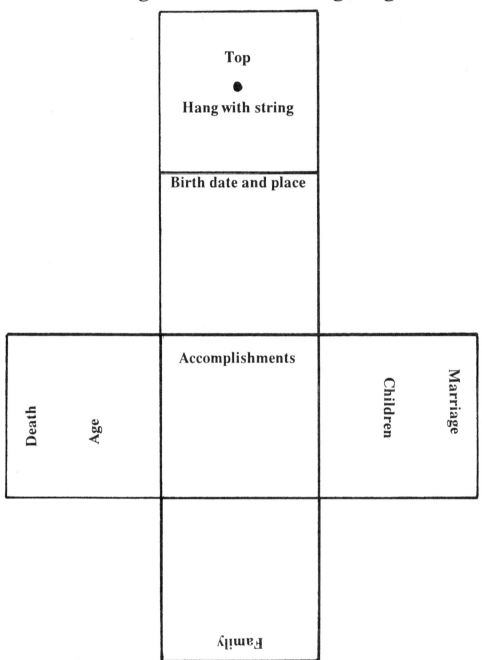

Famous Suffragists List

Susan B. Anthony

Lucretia Mott

Victoria Claflin Woodhull

Emma Goldman

Carrie Chapman Catt

Belva Lockwood

Elizabeth Cady Stanton

Julia Ward Howe

Lucy Stone

Jeannette Rankin

Alice Paul

Francis Willard

Reasons Women Should Vote List

[adapted from the National Woman Suffrage Publishing Co., Inc., ©1910]

1. Those who obey the laws should help to choose those who make the laws.
2. Laws affect women as much as men.
3. Laws which affect women are now passed without consulting them.
4. Laws affecting children should include the woman's point of view as well as the man's.
5. Laws affecting the home are voted on in every session of the Legislature.
6. Women have experience that would be helpful to legislation.
7. To deprive women of the vote is to lower their position in common estimation.
8. Having the vote would increase the sense of responsibility among women toward questions of public importance.
9. Public spirited mothers make public spirited sons.
10. To sum up all reasons in one: "It is for the common good of all."

Fact Sheet

Women's Suffrage — Pro and Con

[adapted from the Albany Branch of New York State Association Opposed To Woman Suffrage]

1. **Pro:** Taxation without representation is tyranny.

   Con: This is an old and tired argument. The reason men vote is not because they pay taxes. Why should women?

2. **Pro:** Women are not citizens because they can't vote.

   Con: The government reasons that women's service to this country is different from men's. Women serve the home and men serve their country. Without homes there would be no country. Therefore, women are just as much citizens of this country as their male counterparts.

3. **Pro:** Women are put in a class of disfranchised citizens the same as criminals, because they have no vote.

   Con: This is the war cry of suffragists. Criminals have been disfranchised by law.

4. **Pro:** Because women are children's caretakers, why shouldn't they have a vote for child welfare laws?

   Con: Laws protecting children come under the National Child Labor Committee. It has nothing to do with women's voting status.

5. **Pro:** There are many working women. Shouldn't they have a right to vote for fair labor conditions?

   Con: There are already excellent labor laws in those manufacturing states that employ women.

6. **Pro:** Laws have been passed about discrimination regarding color, religion, and property. Why should there continue to be discrimination regarding women?

   Con: Men and women are not equal. Government is man's work.

Lesson Plan 9

Auto Racer

OBJECTIVES: To build a metal automobile similar to that with which children played during the second decade of the twentieth century.
To build an object for the Table Top Museum.
To survey people of various ages in order to find out how the popularity of toys has changed.

MATERIALS: For each car: 2 aluminum foil loaf pans (one 5 3/4" x 3 1/4" x 2", one 8" x 3 3/4" x 2 1/2"), heavy corrugated cardboard (for wheels & steering wheel), 4 paper fasteners; glue, tape, scissors, drinking straws, black marker; fact sheet, "The Tin Lizzie;"* illustrations of Tin Lizzie and Metal Toys;* child's wind–up toy car.
*Provided at the end of the lesson.

LENGTH OF TIME: 45 minutes; about 15 minutes time at home before in–class discussion of survey.

PROCEDURE:

1. The teacher holds up a wind–up toy car, demonstrates its use, and asks the students what it is.

2. The teacher tells the students that they will be investigating some of the favorite toys of children at different times during this century. They are to list their own five favorite toys, then ask other people of different ages for their favorites at the same age as they are. They might question an older brother or sister. A parent and a grandparent or older neighbor can also tell their favorite toys. They are to bring the information to the next class.

3. The teacher explains that in the second decade of this century a favorite toy was a model of the Tin Lizzie, a nickname for the mass–produced automobile that Henry Ford built. The teacher distributes the fact sheet, "The Tin Lizzie," and the students read it. The teacher asks questions like the following:

   a. What are some of the reasons that early cars were hard to fix when something went wrong?

   b. Name some of the earliest car manufacturers. (Ford, Dodge, Packard, Hudson, Mawell) Are they all making cars today?

   c. Research the names of other early car manufacturers and the models they made. (Hundred of companies initially made cars. Most did not last.) Your parents or other adults that you know may know the names of other early car makers or models. (Studebaker and Nash are two of the more recent cars that are no longer made. The Edsel made by Ford is an example of a model no longer made.)

d. You may want to ask your parents or grandparents to name all the cars that they have owned. (You will find that most people remember every car that they have ever owned. See if you can find out why.) What has changed about these cars? Where are they made?

5. The students make a replica of a toy car by following the instructions:

a. Use a pencil to incise light lines on left, top, and right sides of the larger loaf pan. (A)

b. Cut through the middle and along the bottoms of the penciled lines. (B)

c. Fold in the sides and fold down the front, making a dashboard. (C)

d. Fold in the sides, and fold up the back, making the seatback. (D)

e. With scissors, shape that seatback. (E)

f. Cut the small aluminum loaf pan in half . Set one half aside. (F)

g. Slide the small loaf pan up, under the seatback of the auto. (G)

h. Staple the sides of the loaf pan to the auto. The seat is now in place. (H)

i. Cut four 3" wheels and one 1 1/2" steering wheel from the cardboard. Darken in wheels, hubs and spokes with black felt tip marker. Attach wheels to auto racer with 4 paper fasteners. (I)

j. With remaining half of small loaf pan, cut 4 wide strips (fenders). Fold each fender lengthwise. Glue along one–half of each fender and attach above each wheel. (J)

k. Cut a paper or plastic drinking straw into a 4" length for the steering column. Use a paper punch to punch out a hole in the middle of the steering wheel. Insert one end of a drinking straw into the steering wheel. Make a tiny slit in the aluminum with the point of a scissors and insert the other end of the drinking straw into the dashboard. (K)

6. At a later class after the students have brought in the results of their toy survey, the teacher places the decades of the twentieth century on the blackboard as headings. As the students have lists of favorite toys from various times during the past century, they put them on the blackboard under the appropriate decade. If the toy is already listed for that decade, the students do not list it again.

7. When the lists are quite extensive, the teacher leads a discussion by asking questions like the following:

a. Which toys were listed in the most decades?

b. How can you account for the popularity of these toys?

c. What generalizations can you make about the toys that children like?

AUTO RACER

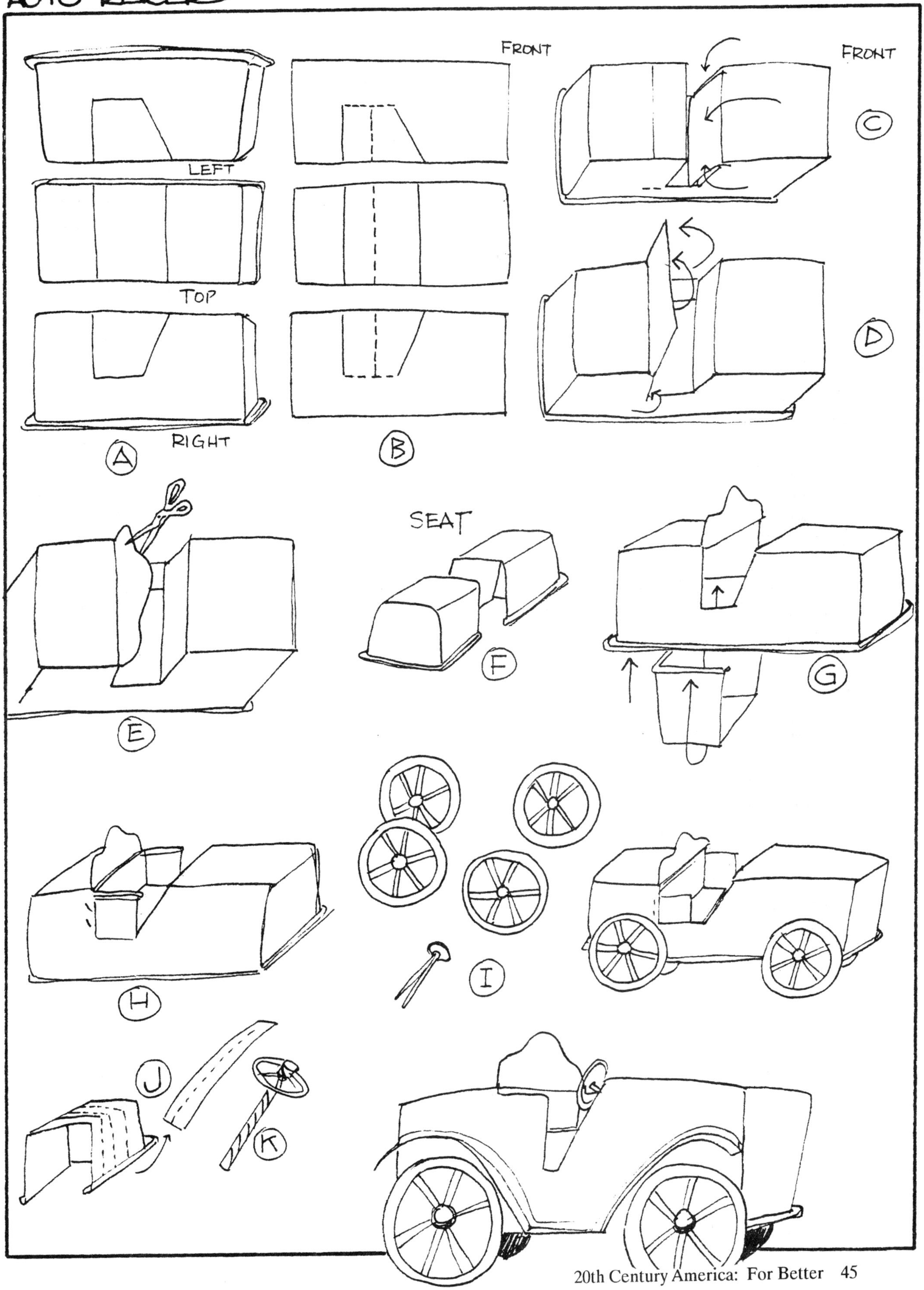

FRONT

FRONT

C

D

LEFT

TOP

RIGHT

A

B

SEAT

E

F

G

H

I

J

K

Fact Sheet

The Tin Lizzie

Automobiles were new and exciting methods of transportation in early 20th century America. Studebaker, previously in the horse–drawn wagon business, began building automobiles in 1902. That same year David D. Buick founded his auto company. But automobiles were very expensive and fickle. Drivers needed tools and equipment to fix any multitude of problems as they rode along.

Henry Ford began experimenting with horseless carriages late in the 19th century. In 1899 he opened an automobile company that soon folded. For a short while he built and raced cars until in 1903 he founded the Ford Motor Company. In just a few years his company was building over half the world's automobiles. In 1910 the Model T cost $850. A few years later with Ford's assembly line production that made identical parts for all the cars, it could be sold for less than half that price. Americans were fascinated with the Ford and everyone wanted one! They were given the nicknames of "Flivver" and "Tin Lizzie." (After 1910 Fords were made from metal rather than wood.)

As the automobile grew in popularity, so did pleasure drives. Sunday rides soon extended into weekend and vacation autocamping trips. Families tied camping equipment to the running boards, started off on a trip, and pulled over anywhere they felt to pitch tents. Problems arose because people often failed to ask permission to camp and left pristine landscapes littered and messy. By 1920 autocamps had sprung up everywhere. These began as campgrounds. Later for a small fee families could drive into autocamp sites and rent small cottages (later called motels). A family of five could drive cross–country, autocamp, and spend only $100 for the whole trip.

Only men drove cars! Doctors stressed that automobiles were too dangerous, and women were too fragile to attempt this vigorous activity. Traveling at speeds of 20 miles an hour would cause sleepless nights, and the recklessness of driving could result in physical and emotional problems, the doctors said. Alice Ramsey, one emancipated woman, drove 4,000 miles from New York City to San Francisco in sixty days and proved the doctors wrong. She was the first woman to drive an automobile across the United States. She found roads were terrible with potholes, rain, mud found, and a lack of maps. She and her three women traveling companions patched tires, roped the car out of mudslides, and jacked it up out of holes. Her last cross–country tour—she made 30 of them—was done at the age of 99. She was honored in 1960 by being named "Woman Motorist of the Century" by the American Manufacturers Association.

Automobiles fascinated children, too. Metal toys, popular during this period, expanded to include simple aeroplanes as well as cars. The "Friction Auto Racer" was an excellent seller. Although a bit pricey (98 cents) it was much more popular than the "Milk Wagon," which sold for 59 cents, horse included.

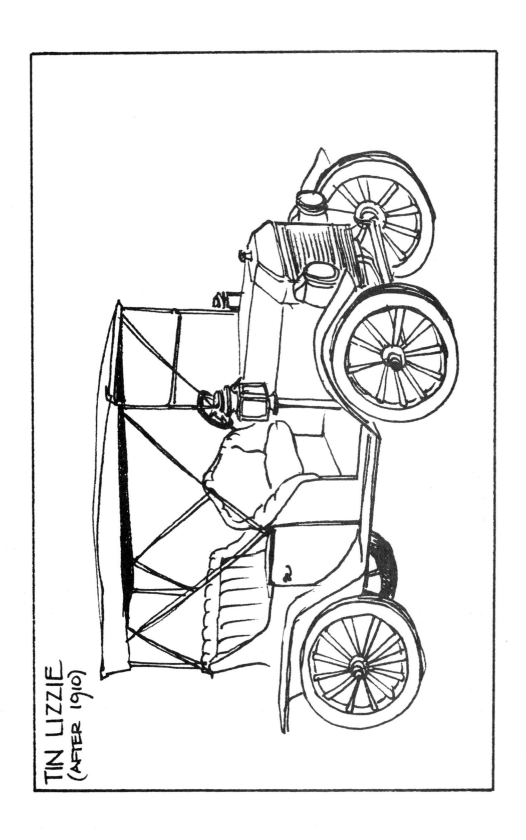

TIN LIZZIE
(AFTER 1910)

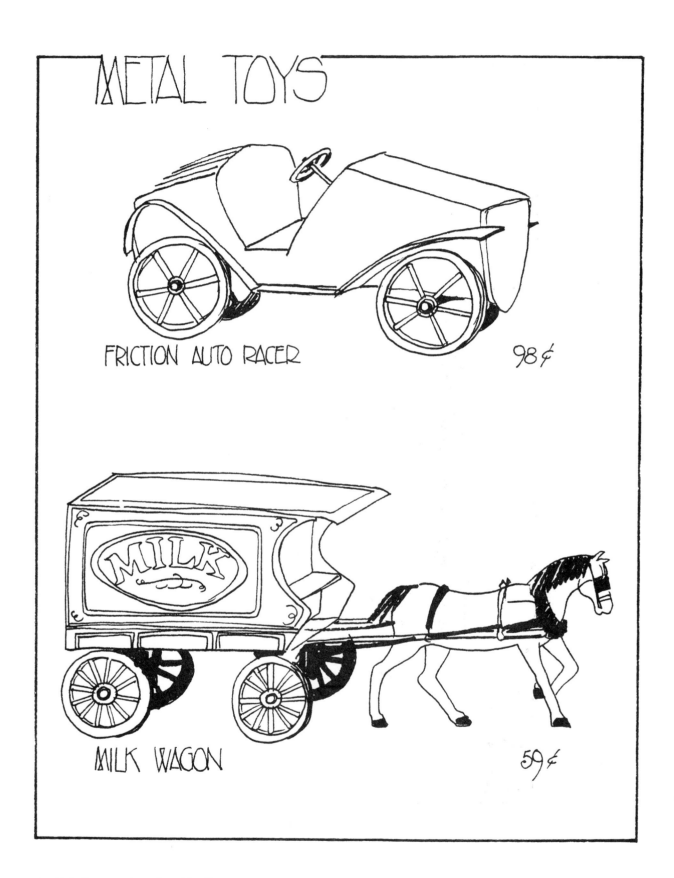

METAL TOYS

FRICTION AUTO RACER   98¢

MILK WAGON   59¢

Lesson Plan 10
Chautauqua Festival

OBJECTIVES: To develop an inspirational program like the Chautauquas.

To present a program to other classrooms or at "A 20th Century America Time Machine."

MATERIALS: Advertisements, banners, posters; costumes (as Chautauqua characters or as festival–goers); props (for Chautauqua characters); references such as Time/Life's *This Fabulous Century — 1910–1920* ; resource on dances and songs of the southwest and the northeast (Suggestions: powwow dance in Perfect–Miller's *Old Settlers/New Settlers in the New World* , 1989; or dances in Doherty's *Indian Lore and Legend,* revised 1993; illustrations: "Chautauqua Characters"* and "Sporting Clothes"*; fact sheet, "Summer Fun."*

*Provided at the end of the lesson.

LENGTH OF TIME: Preparation time: two 45–minute periods; performance time: varies according to number of activities.

PROCEDURE:

1. The teacher asks the students to name the activities they enjoy doing in their leisure time. Based upon what the students now know about the early part of the 20th century, the students check those that they feel people would have enjoyed at an earlier time as well. For example, if the students mention reading, that would have also been enjoyed then, but if they mention television or movies, those would not have yet been popular or even possible.

2. The teacher explains that usually the people had to amuse or entertain themselves, but occasionally another form of entertainment developed and was popular. For example, in western New York State a type of entertainment became popular that was known as a Chautauqua after the area where it was founded. The teacher distributes the fact sheet, "Summer Fun," and the students read it. The teacher asks questions like the following:

   a. What was the main purpose of a Chautauqua?

   b. Why did people enjoy them so much?

   c. Why do you think they included the characters that they did? (Discuss the discrimination that surrounded the Native American.)

   d. Find out why Americans were interested in Hawaii at this time.

3. The teacher explains that the class will stage a Chautauqua for "A 20th Century America Time Machine" and lists on the blackboard the characters and types of entertainment:

SOME CHAUTAUQUA CHARACTERS

NOBLE RED MAN   MAGICIAN   WHOLESOME GIRL

- Announcer—1 needed: The announcer gives a brief explanation of Chautauquas. He or she has a list of performance numbers and names of performers and announces each number.

- College Girls—6 needed: The six girls develop a short skit, a song, or a story told in parts and performed by all six girls.

- Magician with Helper—2 needed: These two individuals research and learn five simple tricks.

- Singing Hawaiian—2 needed: Two students learn and sing a song about or from Hawaii. No dancing girls can be included as this inclusion would be improper.

- Noble Red Man—2 to 4 needed: These individuals research powwow dances and songs of the southwest and the northeast. People playing this character always wore shirts and never were bare–chested as Chautauquas catered to families, and it would have been considered bad taste and very improper for "Noble Red Men" to be partially clothed.

- Band with Bandleader—5 + needed: Prepare two numbers with assistance from your music supervisor. Ask him/her to help you choose musical numbers that were written and performed between 1900 and 1920.

- Gatling Gun—1 needed: Write and present a 2 to 3 minute impassioned speech about "How to Make Money At Home," "Think Positive and Why," or another topic of your choice. Memorize the speech and practice giving it as fast as you can, while still enunciating the words clearly. The person will be billed as "first name Gatling Gun last name." (For example, John Gatling Gun Doe.)

- Characters may be added or deleted, depending on the number of students in the classroom. A whole class performance may travel to other classrooms to deliver their Chautauqua, or festival–goers may be the remaining members of the class or other classrooms and grades.

4. Students take the "Sporting Clothes" illustration home and bring to school any clothing resembling those in the illustration. Men would ordinarily wear sports coats or suits.

Fact Sheet

Summer Fun

Something wonderful happened during America's second decade. Popular summer festivals began traveling through America's hamlets and towns in the form of inspirational tent shows. The first show was put together on Chautauqua Lake in New York State by a group of people who gathered bands, choral groups, magicians, opera singers, yodelers, storytellers, and various interesting people who lectured on inspirational subjects. These shows were a healthy form of family entertainment, and women gladly brought their children. Workshops offered help to beleagued teachers and farmers. Get–rich lectures brought in hopeful crowds. Chautauquas (chaw-TAW-kwaws) eventually grew to week–long festivals traveling through 10,000 American towns, each one drawing around 4,000 visitors.

Back in early 20th century America very little group entertainment was available. Except for the church social or a barn dance or two, families generally entertained themselves. Every summer families counted on these marvelous tent shows that held something for everyone. Stock characters were a native American, called "The Noble Red Man," who performed a ceremonial dance; a singing Hawaiian (America was fascinated with the Hawaiian Islands), accompanying himself on his ukulele; a magician to wow the crowd; and college girls working for the summer who told stories, sang, and danced Irish jigs and other dances. Always present was an inspirational speaker who excited the crowd with tales of money–making ideas or the importance of positive thinking. "Harry Gatling Gun" Fogleman was famous for his 300–words–a–minute speeches. Try it!

Since the summer of 1990, a Chautauqua–like festival has again sprung up. Called "Lollapalooza," this mixture of speeches and music is pulling in crowds just like the Chautauquas of old. Combining concerts, political action exchanges, and alternative music, its intentions are to entertain and to provoke people to think about their lives. Lollapaloozas are one–day events attracting between 30,000 and 40,000 people to their mixture of mohawks and mosh pits for body–slamming or bumping where young people gather to question, buy interesting trinkets, dance, and enjoy the music.

Do you see similarities between these two festivals? Ninety years separate them in musical styles and politics, but the general idea is the same. Bring 'em in, entertain 'em, and get 'em thinking. They are open forums where people give their opinions, generate ideas, and become conscious of whom they are.

Lesson Plan 11
Let's Make A Radio!

OBJECTIVE: To build a radio for the "Table Top Museum" or for "A 20th Century America Time Machine."

MATERIALS: Fact sheet, "World War I;"* paper towel cardboard tube, germanium diode, earphone with wire leads, 35 feet of #22 gauge insulated wire, hole-punch, sandpaper, scissors (or wire-stripper), 2 alligator clips; encyclopedia, *World Almanac*; example of grid*; "Decision-Making Process Sheet."*
*Provided at the end of the lesson.

SPECIAL INSTRUCTIONS: The radios made by the class are simple ones that will be effected by time of day, weather conditions, and proximity of radio stations. Reception will be better at night when those stations remaining on the air are required to be more directional with their antennas causing less interference with each other. Reception improves with proximity to the broadcasting station.

The needed equipment can be purchased at an electronics store like Radio Shack. The cost for these radios is small—germanium diodes are about 10 for one dollar.

The germanium crystal was used in radios at the time of World War I. The diode results in better reception. Galena crystals, sometimes used in crystal radio kits, are less sensitive.

LENGTH OF TIME: About 1 hour.

PROCEDURE:

1. The teacher asks the students to make a list of the different ways people communicate over distance with each other today. Which of the ways they have mentioned could have been used in the 1920's? (Students may need to research some of their ideas.) The teacher explains that communication became extremely important during World War I.

2. The fact sheet, "World War I," is distributed and read. The teacher can determine the students' understanding of the fact sheet by asking questions like the following:

   a. What is an ally?

   b. What are some of the situations that may make countries allies of each other?

   c. Why would a war change the way women were viewed by the country?

3. The class is divided into groups of four or five students, and each group makes a decision about which communication method that was available would have been best to use in the military in World War I. The decision-making process is reviewed by looking at the "Decision-Making Process Sheet." Each group lists the various communication methods across the top of a grid and the criteria that they decide upon down the

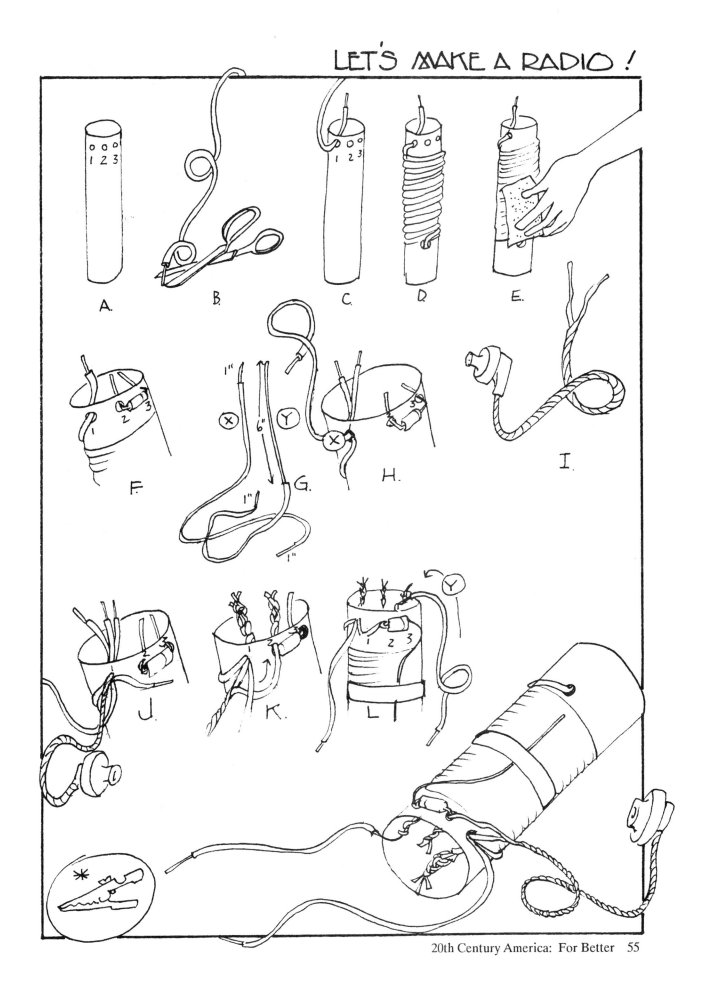

left–hand side of the grid. (See grid for example.) The teacher may wish to review the criteria with each group for appropriateness.

4. The groups rate each method against the criteria using a numerical system, then decide which methods would have been best for use by the military in World War I.

5. Whether or not the students come with radio as their first choice, the teacher explains that radios were essential equipment during World War I. Women knew how to work them, how to repair them, and how to put them together. The students will make a simple radio using modern day materials. They are to follow the instructions:

    a. Punch 3 holes in the cardboard tube. Punch about 1" apart near the top (A).

    b. Cut six feet off the 35–foot insulated wire. Put the six–foot piece aside. Strip off 1" of insulation from one end of the long length (29–foot piece) of wire. (B)

    c. Insert this end that has been stripped of insulation through hole #1. (C)

    d. Carefully wrap the rest of the long wire around the tube. Be careful not to overlap the wire. Make a hole in the tube at the other end where the wire ends. Insert the wire in the hole to make a clean end. (D)

    e. Use coarse sandpaper to sand off the middle length of insulated coils. Carefully sand a strip from top to bottom until you see the wire under the insulation. (E)

    f. Place the ends of the germanium diode into hole 2 and hole 3. Bend the wires to keep them in place. (F) NOTE: If the germanium diode is painted on one end, put that end through Hole 3 and attach to wire Y (see "g").

    g. Take the 6–foot wire that was set aside. Cut it in half (Length X and Length Y). Strip 1" of insulation off both ends of Length X. Strip 1" of insulation off one end and 6" off the other end of length Y. (G)

    h. Take wire length X and insert one end through hole 1. There are now **2** wires in hole 1. (H)

    i. Strip 1" of insulation off the ends of the wires attached to the earphone. (I)

    j. Insert one earphone wire through hole 1. (J)

    k. Twist the ends of all three wires together – hole 1. (K)

    l. Insert the other earphone wire through hole 2. Twist this wire around the diode wire in hole 2. (K)

    m. Place the long–stripped end of wire Y inside the tube and insert out through hole 3. Twist the diode wire around some of the bare wire inside. Lay the remaining bare wire down the side of the sandpapered exposed wire and attach a rubber band around the tube to hold the wire in place (L)

    n. Attach alligator clips to the bare ends of wires X and Y outside the tube (bottom illustration).

6. The teacher explains to the students that to use the radio they need to attach either the X wire or the Y wire to a "ground" such as a metal radiator or a faucet and attach the other wire to an antenna. The better the antenna, the better the reception will be.

Students can even be the antenna on this simple radio by holding the end of the wire between their fingers. When the antenna is hooked up, the earphone is put in the listener's ear. Then the end of wire X is moved slowly across the exposed coiled wire on the tube until a station is heard. Once a station is heard, the rubber band is put on to hold the "tuner" in place.

Example of Decision–Making Grid

	Horn	Drum	Telephone	Radio	Telegraph
Criterion 1 Carries sound over a long distance	3	3	5	5	5
Criterion 2 Lightweight, easy to carry	2	1	3	4	4
Criterion 3 Easy to repair	4	2	2	2	2
Criterion 4 Inexpensive to use	5	5	3	4	3
Criterion 5 Easy to learn to use	4	5	5	5	3
Criterion 6 Doesn't require lines or cables	5	5	1	5	1
Total	23	21	19	25	18

In this example, the radio had the highest number of points. Alternatively, the person filling out the grid can be required to rank each use for the criterion, that is, use each number once in a horizontal row. Additional criteria can be added if 3–5 fail to discriminate sufficently. Also note that some criteria are better than others in their discriminatory capacity.

In this sample, 1 = meets criterion hardly at all; 2 = meets criterion a little bit; 3 = meets criterion fairly well; 4 = meets criterion quite well; 5 = meets criterion extrememly well.

Decision–Making Process Sheet

1. Describe the conditions of World War I that might require communication. List one of them.

2. List the obstacles that exist in the situation.

3. Make a list of possible solutions to the problems. Write them across the top of a grid.

4. Establish criteria to follow in deciding which solution will be picked. Place these criteria down one side of the grid.

5. Make a decision using the criteria by assigning numerical values to the solutions. State what the decision is.

6. Give reasons for picking the solution that you select. State how your decision meets each of the criteria that you listed.

World War I

Serbia and Bosnia were in the news back in the early part of the 20th Century just as they are today. Back then these two small states were among several that were ruled by a country called Austria–Hungary. Great Britain was nervous about Germany. France, too, had problems with Germany. As tensions grew, countries began developing alliances with like–minded countries.

In 1914, after Archduke Ferdinand, heir to the throne of Austria–Hungary, was assassinated by Serbs. Austria–Hungary declared war on Serbia. Immediately, France and England (the Allies) got behind Serbia. Germany sided with Austria–Hungary (the Central Powers). War was on in Europe.

The United States tried to stay neutral. It was difficult because America—the Melting Pot—was the home of people of many nationalities. Some had German sympathies, while others felt a strong tie with England and France. The torpedoing and sinking of the passenger liner "Luistania" in 1915 by a German U–boat was a great push toward U.S. involvement in the war. One hundred twenty eight Americans were killed. President Woodrow Wilson, however, still held out for non–involvement until he learned of a secret plot by Germany to get Mexico to attack the United States. War against the Central Powers was declared by Congress on April 2, 1917.

Women in World War I

Today over 200,000 women serve in the United States military, but prior to World War I women were not allowed to serve—at least as military personnel. Nurses in World War I were civilians whom the Army hired. When the U.S. entered World War I, women were finally allowed to join up. In the Navy they were allowed to enlist as yeoman(F)—yeoman/female where they served as clerks. Twelve thousand women joined up and trained as telegraph operators, radio repairmen, and switchboard operators. Women who stayed at home often worked in munitions factories where they toiled on assembly lines.

Women also worked at a variety of other things to help the war effort. They served in the American Red Cross, which employed hospital units, canteen services, and ambulance corps. Women made food boxes for captured Americans, worked in refugee shelters, and developed the Home Service that helped military families back home. Even the children helped in the war effort by doing things like knitting socks. A Junior Red Cross for kids was formed.

As American men marched off to war, women took their places in jobs traditionally reserved for men. Women became auto mechanics, streetcar conductors, farmers, and policemen. They were working outside the home, helping in the war effort, making a change in America's economy, and changing their lives in so many ways that America would always look at them in a different light.

Bibliography

1900–1910

Allen, Frederick Lewis. *The Big Change: America Transforms Itself 1900–1950*. New York: Torchbooks, Harper & Row, 1988.

A good picture of the strong class differences in early 20th century America.

Bales, C.A. *Tales of the Elders: A Memory Book of Men and Women Who Came to America as Immigrants, 1900–1930*. New York: Follett, 1977.

Great photographic account of immigrants coming to this country in the early 20th Century.

Beller, Susan Provost. *Roots for Kids*. Box 219, Crozet, VA 22932, Betterway Publications, Inc. 1989.

This genealogy guide/activity book is based on a 12–week course the author developed for her fourth grade class.

Blum, N.A. *Everyday Fashions of the Twenties*. New York: Dover, 1990.

_____. *Everyday Fashions of the Thirties*. New York: Dover, 1991.

The two Blum books contain clothing pictured in Sears and other catalogs. Dover also reprints Gimbel Brothers' *1915 Fashion Catalog, Women's Fashions of the Early 1900's* from National Cloak & Suit Co., and a new title by Olian, *Everyday Fashions of the Forties as Pictured in Sears Catalogs*. Interested teachers can write to Dover at 31 East 2nd Street, Mineola, NY 11501 for a complete price list of these and other fashion books.

Burns, Olive Ann. *Cold Sassy Tree*. New York: Bantam Doubleday Dell, 1984.

Excellent depiction of life in a small southern town in 1906.

Chorzempa, Rosemary. *My Family Tree Workbook*. New York: Dover, 1989.

Younger students can record information on three generations of their family in this workbook.

Dionetti, Michelle. *Coal Mine Peaches*. New York: Orchard Books, 1991.

A young girl's grandfather tells stories of his native Italy, how he came to New York to help build the Brooklyn Bridge, and work in the coal mines.

Encyclopedia Britannica, Inc. *The Annals of America*. Chicago, IL, 1976.

"Employments Unsuitable for Women" by Henry T. Finck; opposing view: "Women Ought to Work" by Ida Husted Harper.

Freedman, Russell. *Immigrant Kids*. New York: E.P. Dutton, 1980.

Good look at the life of immigrant children at school, home, work, and play in New York City during the early 1900's.

Fisher, L.E. *Ellis Island*. New York: Holiday House, 1986.

Focus is on immigrant processing at Ellis Island.

Fritz, Jean. *Bully for You, Teddy Roosevelt!* New York: G.P Putnam's Sons, 1991.

An excellent biography of our twenty–sixth President.

Hartley, E.F. *Clues to American Dress*. Washington, D.C.: Elliott and Clark, 1991.

Covers nearly four centuries of clothing worn by the average American woman.

Harvey, B. *Immigrant Girl: Becky of Eldridge Street*. New York: Holiday House, 1987.

Becky, a Russian Jew, comes to America to escape persecution and lives in 1910 New York City.

Katz, William Loren & Jacqueline Hunt. *Making Our Way: America at the Turn of the Century in the Words of the Poor and Powerless*. NY, Dial Press, 1975.

This Junior Literary Guild selection tells what life was like for the coal miner, the shop girl, the hobo, and many other ordinary people living in America at the turn of the century.

Koral, April. *An Album of The Great Wave of Immigration*. New York: Franklin Watts, 1992.

A pictorial history of the great immigration wave that occurred from 1890 to 1924.

Leighton, Maxinne Rhea. *An Ellis Island Christmas*. New York: Viking, 1992.

Krysia and her family leave Poland to join her father in the U.S. On Christmas Eve they steam into New York harbor and see the Statue of Liberty.

Levoy, Myron. *The Witch of Fourth Street and Other Stories*. New York: HarperCollins, 1972.

A charming book of short stories about various immigrant families living in and around Second Avenue in New York City. Irish, Italian, Greek and Lithuanian families know and help each other as they all seek to find a better life in America.

Mayerson, E.W. *The Cat Who Escaped From Steerage*. New York: Scribner, 1990.

A nine year–old girl, traveling to America in steerage, finds a cat and carries it to America.

McDonald, Megan. *The Potato Man*. New York: Orchard Books, 1991.

A story of early 20th Century urban America about a scary–looking peddler and a young boy.

Pellowski, Anne. *The Family Storytelling Handbook*. New York: Macmillan, 1987.

How to use stories, anecdotes, rhymes, and realia to enrich your family traditions.

Perl, Lila. *The Great Ancestor Hunt: The Fun of Finding Out Who You Are.* New York: Clarion Books, 1989.

Details on how to create your own ancestry chart, how to conduct family interviews and how to write away for public records.

Seeger, Pete & Reiser, Bob. *Carry It On: The Story of America's Working People in Song and Picture.* Bethlehem, PA: Sing Out Publications, 1991.

1900–1918 songs about immigrants; child labor; miners ("Babes in the Mill", "A Miner's Life"); unions; African Americans; automakers; farmers ("Black, Brown, and White Blues", "Mine Eyes Have Seen the Glories of the Making of a Ford", "I am A Union Woman"), and the destitute ("The Soup Song").

Shiman, David A. *The Prejudice Book: Activities for the Classroom.* 823 United nations Plaza, New York: Anti–Defamation League of the B'nai B'rith, 1979.

A series of activities that help children deal with conflicts and tensions that emerge in a pluaristic society.

TIME/LIFE Books. *This Fabulous Century: 1900–1910.* Alexandria, VA: Time–Life Books, 1987.

Lots of information—from "Flying Machines" to "A Woman's Place and the Immigrants' Ordeal."

Tunnell, Michael O. & Ammon, Richard, Ed. *The Story of Ourselves: Teaching History Through Children's Literature.* Portsmouth, NH: Heinemann, 1993.

Marvelously innovative activities (for Immigration: "Decision–Making using age in a pluralistic society.

TIME/LIFE Books. *This Fabulous Century: 1900–1910.* Alexandria, VA: Time–Life Books, 1987.

Lots of information—from "Flying Machines" to "A Woman's Place and the Immigrants' Ordeal."

Tunnell, Michael O. & Ammon, Richard, Ed. *The Story of Ourselves: Teaching History Through Children's Literature.* Portsmouth, NH: Heinemann, 1993.

Marvelously innovative activities (for Immigration: "Decision–Making using a Decision Tree") and a superb, annotated bibliography covering many aspects of American history.

Magazines

Cobblestone. "American Immigration Part I," Vol. 3, #12, December, 1982.

_____. "American Immigration Part II," Vol. 4, #1, January, 1983.

Films

An American Tail (1986) and *An American Tail—Fievel Goes West* (1991). Video available of both. Rated G, Dom DeLuise.

Younger children will enjoy this animated film of immigrant mice coming to the United States at the end of the 19th century.

Far and Away (1992). Video available. Rated PG–13, Tom Cruise.

The very beginning of this film shows Irish immigrants coming to Boston and what they encounter. It is set in the 1890's but might be helpful.

1910–1920

Balliett, Whitney. *Jelly Roll, Jabbo & Fats: 19 Portraits in Jazz.* New York: Oxford University Press, 1983.

Written by the famed jazz critic of *The New Yorker*, this book covers well–known jazz musicians beginning with Jelly Roll Morton; excellent short biographies.

Brady, Kathleen. *Ida Tarbell: Portrait of a Muckraker.* New York: Seaview/Putnam, 1984.

A wonderful resource book for teachers to understand more clearly not only the position of women from the late 19th century but also the development of a women's rights activist during that time.

Boydston, Jeanne; Kelley, Mary; and Margolis, Anne. *The Limits of Sisterhood: The Beecher Sisters on Women's Rights and Women's Sphere.* Chapel Hill, NC: University of North Carolina Press, 1988.

Excellent resource that covers the three Beecher sisters and the influence of each on the role of women in America. Great background material on Isabella and her views on women's suffrage.

Golden Owl Portfolio. *Band Music in American Life: A Social History 1850-1990.* P.O. Box AO3, Amawalk, NY: Golden Owl Publishing Co., 1992.

Primary resource material (including audio tape) on music in early 20th Century America.

Doherty, Edith J.S. *Indian Lore and Legend.* East Windsor Hill, CT: Synergetics, 1993.

The dances in this book can be used when staging a Chautauqua.

Gurko, Miriam. *The Ladies of Seneca Falls: The Birth of the Woman's Rights Movement.* New York: Macmillan Publishing Co., Inc. 1974.

Good background material about the beginnings of the woman's rights movement.

Jackdaws No. P22. *Votes for Women: The Fight for Suffrage.* Box A03, Amawalk, NY: Jackdaws Inc., 1992.

Primary resource material includes cartoons and handbills; "Be Good to California, Mr. Wilson" sheet music, 1916; news excerpts; and an early publication by Susan B. Anthony.

Jacobs, W.J. *Mother, Aunt Susan and Me: The First Fight for Women's Rights*. New York: Coward, 1979.

Historical fiction. The young daughter of Elizabeth Cady Stanton tells the story of the struggle for women's rights.

Mills, Lauren. *The Rag Coat*. Boston: Little, Brown & Co., 1991.

Fictional account of a young Applachian girl and her new coat, made by scrap pieces carefully chosen because of the stories behind them.

Oneal, Z. *A Long Way To Go*. New York: Viking Press, 1990.

The story of an eight year–old girl who deals with women's suffrage during World War I.

Perfect–Miller, Suzanne. *Old and New Settlers in the New World*. East Windsor Hill, CT: Synergetics, 1991.

The dances in this book can be incorporated into a Chautauqua.

Sullivan, George. The Day the Women Got the Vote: A Photo History of the Women's Rights Movement. New York: Scholastic, 1994.

Text and black and white photos covering the period from the mid–nineteenth century until today. Excellent coverage of women's suffrage, suffragists, dress reform, and women in wars.

TIME/LIFE Books. *This Fabulous Century — 1910–1920*. Alexandria, VA: Time/Life Books, 1969.

Includes changes in women's roles, movies, culture; covers WW I through the madcap roaring 20's and all its crazes.

Magazines

Cobblestone. "U.S. Involvement in World War I," Vol. 7, #6, June, 1986.

_____. "Cobblestone Hits the Road: The Automobile in History," Vol. 8, #7, July, 1987.

Films

The Great Gatsby (1974). Video available. Rated PG.

Shows prohibition and the Age of Jazz.

The Sinking of the Lusitania (1918). No video available. No rating.

An animated recreation of the event. This documentary is considered to be the first successful attempt at animation.

EDUCATION LIBRARY
DUNCAN McARTHUR HALL
QUEEN'S UNIVERSITY
KINGSTON, ONTARIO
K7L 3N6

D1370849

20th CENTURY AMERICA

FOR WORSE

The Plunging Twenties

The Depressed Thirties

Suzanne Perfect–Miller

SYNERGETICS

REACHING THROUGH TEACHING

E741.P47 1994

© 1994 by Suzanne Perfect–Miller

For teacher use in a school, classroom quantities of student–pages may be duplicated.
The reproduction of any part for an entire school, school system, or for commercial use is
prohibited. Published by Synergetics,® P.O. Box 84, East Windsor Hill, CT 06028.

ISBN 0–945984–71–5

Table of Contents

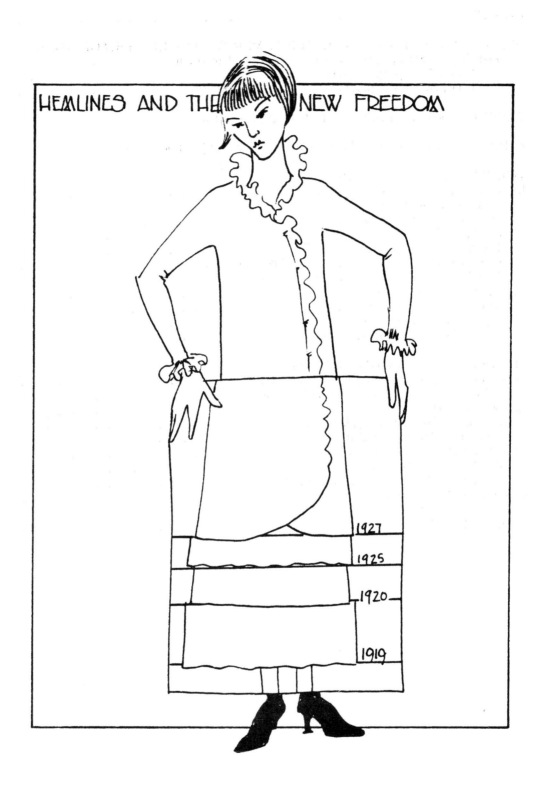

HEMLINES AND THE NEW FREEDOM

1927

1925

1920

1919

Introduction

If you were living during the twenties and thirties you would be seeing years of tremendous change in America. World War I had disillusioned Americans and they became determined to focus on their own country. For a while they felt the dread of creeping communism. Feeling that the big corporations were squeezing the labor force with inadequate pay and poor working conditions, the Labor movement started massive strikes un retaliation. The coal and steel industries were hardest hit by these strikes. The working people listened to the intellectuals who voiced their own disillusionment. Angry and rebellious young people set out to make their own rules and to defy convention. They were ready for revolt. Would you join with these young people by becoming one of those "wild" flappers of the twenties?

Airplanes, closed automobiles, radios, modern appliances, Freudian thought, miniature golf, and marathon dancing added to your new freedom. Could anything go wrong? Speculation in the stock market merely added to the frenzied excitement as people played on margin and giddily dove into the deep end of the pool.

The stock market crash of 1929 wiped many people out and was sobering to lots more. What happened? Did they see it coming? How long would it take America to recover?

Nature failed to help. Drought in the midwest turned lush farmlands into an overwhelming dustbowl, forcing farmers to pull up stakes and leave. "Oakies" and "Arkies" loaded their exhausted families into patched–up cars and headed for the vineyards and citrus groves of California. Did they find a better life? Would they find acceptance?

What happened to Americans during these early decades? How did they survive the changes? How did music influence them? How did they live through the Depression? Did children really ride the rails, rubbing elbows with hobos?

An excellent way to understand change as it happened to two diverse groups of people is to roleplay their lives—all described and illustrated in detail in the pages of this unique combination of two how–to handbooks in one:

20th Century America: For Better

Immigration 1900–1910

Women's Worlds 1910–1920

and

20th Century America: For Worse

The Plunging Twenties, 1920–1930

The Depressed Thirties, 1930–1940

For *20th Century America: For Better*, please turn over the book. For *20th Century America: For Worse*, please turn the page....

Ways of Presenting 20th Century America — For Worse: Planning A 20th Century Time Machine

This book gives instructions for dancing the Charleston, planting trees and gardens under the WPA program, presenting a round table discussion at the Algonquin Hotel, buting stock on margin, developing characters of famous people, learning language terms of the "flappers," building costumes, roleplaying 30's life, and painting a mural as part of the Federal Artists' Project. These activities can be presented in a variety of ways depending upon the teacher's objectives, the abilities and interests of the students, and the particular facilities of the school. Preparation time for the program takes approximately 6 weeks.

One interesting way to present *FOR WORSE* is to divide the class into the "Plunging Twenties" and the "Depressed Thirties." Each side prepares projects and programs of the decade that it is studying. In this way, students from each group become familiar with the problems (and solutions) the two decades faced.

A second way of presenting *FOR WORSE* is used if one grade consists of more than one classroom. In this case, each room in that grade becomes the eras of the 20's or the 30's. The students create a decade of special projects — for example, organize a corporation, roleplay a highbrow at the Algonquin Round Table, or paint a mural through the WPA program. A target date could be established for "A Twenties and Thirties Night" with invitations sent to other grades and parents.

I prefer "A 20th Century America Time Machine," an event that incorporates both handbooks of *20th Century America: For Better/For Worse*. "A 20th Century America Time Machine" is best presented outdoors in the spring or fall as an evening or weekend activity and includes townspeople, parents, and friends. It can also be presented in the cafeteria or gymnasium. The program's events include a parade of characters; displays; a Chautauqua Festival; and a schedule of dramatic events, exhibits, and performances.

How to Set up the Program

Visitors travel back in time to the turn of the century where they encounter immigrants passing through Ellis Island and are welcomed by the Time Machine Captain. Tables and benches are set up as students roleplay their characters in the activity. America comes to life as visitors view New York City tenements and watch as immigrants from many nationalities and cultures work together to outwit their unscrupulous landlord. As we move into the second decade, women take an important place in America's history. We attend a Women's Suffrage Rally, observe a display of Tin Lizzies, discover women's role in World War I as we see how radios are made, and attend a Chautauqua Festival. As we move into the twenties, we experience a whole new attitude — America is going wild! We meet famous people, listen to the amazing 20's lingo, and get a peek at the Algonquin Round Table group, which is in high gear. We watch students dance the Charleston. We listen to a growing company talk about high finance and learn what happens when the

Stock Market crashes in 1929. Moving into the thirties, we see what depression has done to everyone. We walk past Hoovervilles, Oakievilles, and hobo jungles. We hear the plaintive song of hopelessness in "Brother, Can You Spare a Dime?" We see the effects of dust storms and scorched earth when we look at the corn crops in the Dust Bowl. And we see hope as we view projects from Roosevelt's New Deal — the WPA Artists Project and the CCC Community Beautification project.

How to Schedule the Events

Visitors move to one end of the gymnasium or playing field to the sign marked "1900–1910." Students in appropriate costume move through the "Ellis Island Experience." Following that activity, the next group of students performs the creative drama, "Mrs. Dunn's Loverly, Loverly Farm."

Visitors move to the sign marked "1910–1920." Here they are treated to a rally and a Chautauqua Festival. They view student–built exhibits of products produced during this period.

Past the sign marked "1920–1930," elegantly dressed students roam about and, as the music begins, dance a spirited Charleston. Several move on to the Algonquin Round Table where we're treated to barbed innuendo and outrageous wit.

Next, a narrator explains the beginnings of jazz, and we hear a call and response activity, in the vocabulary of the 20's. We walk to a group of businessmen explaining how they started their company and, to everyone's horror, the shout of "CRASH." The Stock Market has CRASHED!

Under the sign marked "1930–1940," we see nothing but poverty and hopelessness. Students sit in front of makeshift shelters. Some panhandle. Some stand in breadlines. As we walk through a breadline, we are handed homemade bread. Several people step forward and give us apples. We note that they wear signs that say "Unemployed. Buy Apples. 5 cents." We hear their song and we listen to their stories. Last, we see programs from Roosevelt's New Deal — murals on school grounds and a school/community conservation effort.

Events are consecutive beginning with 1900. The audience moves forward through each decade. Each group of students remain in their places after finishing their programs. Allow about 30 minutes for each decade.

9:00–9:30   Immigration sequence

9:30–10:00   Women's Worlds sequence

10:00–10:30   Plunging Twenties sequence

10:30–11:00   Depressed Thirties sequence

To help the audience enjoy and become part of the program, a hand–out prepared by one of the tabletop museum groups gives a brief summary of the scheduled events.

Background Information for the Teacher

The Plunging Twenties: 1920–1930

Everybody was tired—tired of the effects of war and of being the world's caretaker; tired of long, hard hours in jobs that brought little pay; and sick and tired of just plain worry. First there had been the responsibility of World War I and our involvement in it. After the War defense plants closed and people were jobless. The stock market went down. The Red Scare (communism) bubbled and spewed in the background and people thought it was creeping into every nook and cranny. This unrestful period strengthened the power of the Ku Klux Klan and other fringe organizations. Coal and steel strikes shook the foundations of America as workers struggled to get better pay and better working conditions. They'd won the war! Now it was time to straighten out the country!

It was time to take care of themselves and have some fun. The twenties ushered in all sorts of amusements and distractions. This was the time for the "highbrows" who through their writings and discussions changed forever Victorian attitudes and customs. It was a time to become free of straitlaced ideas. Time to be free! Just take a look at the hemlines to get an idea of how things were changing. The shorter the skirts, the more open and radical the country was becoming. Lots of people were appalled by this new thinking. Bills were introduced to reform women's clothing. In Utah, a bill was introduced to send women to jail if their skirts were higher than three inches above the ankle!

For many women, home was no longer the focus for the family. Modern appliances and "bought" canned goods got women out of the kitchens. More and more women joined the workforce and were getting an equal voice.

The twenties introduced the speakeasy and cocktail party (despite the 18th prohibition amendment), the 5 & 10 cent store, crossword puzzles, paved roads and gas stations, "plus fours" and argyle socks, the Charleston, barnstorming, Mah Jong, beauty pageants, "Lucky Lindy," installment plans, and stock market speculation.

Scandals like the Teapot Dome oil scandal and the Veterans' Bureau fraud under Charles R. Forbes developed. Gangsters and the "Mob" ruled whole areas of life in many cities. (The St. Valentine Day Massacre occurred in 1929 in Chicago and killed 7 rival gangsters.) The Scopes ("Monkey") trial and the Sacco and Vanzetti trial were in the news. Everyone was going blotto over cheap, available radios, and sports, sports, sports! People followed the World Series with Babe Ruth; horse racing with their favorite, Man 'O War; and prize fighters, especially Jack Dempsey. Golf became a game of politics and business as meetings were conducted on the course. Young men and women partied and wore outrageous clothing. Women bobbed their hair and insisted on being unchaperoned on outings and at parties. Highbrows—the artists, writers, and poets—wrote and criticized, voicing their disappointment with America. The country heard their outcry and responded.

Many people who became famous household names (and a few who became infamous)

date to the 1920's. Aviators, theater people, mobsters, writers, jazz musicians, and politicians joined the highbrows in putting the 20's on the map. Below is a list of such personages whose lives students might like to roleplay:

Eddie Rickenbacker	Amelia Earhart	Charles Lindbergh
Calbraith Perry Rogers	Harriet Quimby	Wiley Post
Casey Jones	Ethel Waters	Bill "Bojangles" Robinson
Bessie Smith	Joe Oliver	Louis Armstrong
Duke Ellington	George Gershwin	Al Capone
Henry Cabot Lodge	Edna St. Vincent Millay	H.L. Mencken
Langston Hughes	Eugene O'Neill	Sinclair Lewis
Richard Byrd	Will Rogers	William Jennings Bryan
Clarence Darrow	Greta Garbo	Rudolph Valentino
Douglas Fairbanks	Charlie Chaplin	Clara Bow
Red Grange	Babe Ruth	Jack Dempsey
Calvin Coolidge	Warren Harding	FDR
Einstein	Scott Joplin	F. Scott Fitzgerald
Zelda	Dr. Robert H. Goddard	Al Jolson

The Depressed Thirties: 1930–1940

Even if an individual had avoided the stock market, he or she was ultimately affected by the stock market crash. As the decade started off, almost 80 percent of America was living close to the bone, whether they were on a farm in the Midwest, making cars in Detroit, or operating a small store in Philadelphia or New York City. People got by, lived from paycheck to paycheck, and had few extras.

Famous political figures, business people, writers, musicians, sports figures, and actors of the period included:

Herbert Hoover	Andrew Mellon	FDR
Eleanor Roosevelt	William Randolph Hearst	George M. Cohan
John Steinbeck	Ben Shahn	Sophie Tucker
Elsa Maxwell	Joan Crawford	Alfred G. Vanderbilt
Cole Porter	Barbara Hutton	John L. Lewis
Judy Garland	Bette Davis	"Pet Hates" Ball
Clark Gable	Claudette Colbert	Jean Harlow
Marlene Dietrich	W.C. Fields	Mae West
Huey Long	Duke Ellington	Count Basie
Benny Goodman	Billie Holliday	Ella Fitzgerald

Pearl Buck   Huey Long   Margaret Mitchell

George Gershwin   Thomas Wolfe   William Faulkner

Big business kept getting bigger — developing more products yet keeping wages low. New technology meant better, more efficient machines that required fewer people to run them. As a result the average worker couldn't afford to buy the products he made. Something had to give!

World War I had kept farmers busy. They grew crops and raised livestock to feed and clothe Americans and Europeans alike. They built more silos, grain warehouses, and barns to keep up with the demands of more production. When the war ended, they kept up the large production in order to pay the bills and debts that they had incurred during expansion. A surplus of crops and livestock was inevitable and as a result prices plummeted.

The law of supply and demand no longer worked. Nobody was able to buy the ever–increasing supply of goods. Some big businesses could swallow the losses, but small mom–and–pop stores and shops simply couldn't make ends meet as, one by one, they began to close down. Street after street in cities and towns across America had its boarded–up storefronts, breadlines, eviction notices, and Hoovervilles built in parks and under bridges.

Bank failure, bankruptcy, unemployment, poverty, homelessness, as a feeling of hopelessness slowly spread everywhere. Some schools even closed due to insufficient funds, others cut back on books and supplies. Teachers worked for a fraction of their salaries — sometimes up to a 50% reduction in pay. Lots of children simply walked away, finding jobs in sweatshops, farms, or factories to supplement their family income. Child labor laws went out the window. Other children headed out to points south and west. They hopped freight trains, picking up work where they could, and living among the hobos in camps called "jungles." The Children's Bureau figured that by mid–decade over 125,000 children under the age of 21 were wandering around the country.

As the Depression deepened people reached further into their pockets. Surely this couldn't last! They used up their savings. Then they sold the furniture and pawned the jewelry. Many lost their homes. Furniture and cars bought on installment plans were repossessed. Eviction was common.

President Hoover believed in "rugged individualism" where everybody worked out their own problems. It soon became "ragged individualism," and he became the brunt of jokes:

- Hoover blanket: old newspapers used as coverings for people sleeping on park benches.
- Hoover flags: pocket linings pulled out to show nothing inside.
- Hoover hogs: rabbits caught for food.
- Hoover wagons: broken down vehicles that were pulled by mules.

- Hoovervilles: vacant lots where the homeless built cardboard and scrap metal shelters.
- Hoover hotels: flophouses where people could get food and a place to sleep.

To make things worse, nature joined the fitful and plunging economy with an unprecedented drought that broke the backs of farmers in America's midsection. Those who lived in the Panhandle – land covering Kansas, Oklahoma, Texas and New Mexico – were hit the worst. These "dry farmers" (so–called because rain was the only water supply they had to irrigate their crops) grew corn and wheat and raised livestock. Dry weather ushered in the thirties. It wouldn't rain! Farmers who were already overwhelmed by the Great Depression watched their crops dry up and their livestock starve until, one by one, they lost their farms to the banks.

Everything dried up. Then the winds came and blew and blew for four long years leaving the great Dust Bowl that covered the Oklahoma Panhandle, Kansas, Nebraska, Colorado, Texas, and New Mexico. It carried away much of the topsoil, leaving nothing but cracked clay. Farmers had failed to practice crop rotation or use cover crops in the winter. They now tried different planting techniques and different crops. But it was all in vain. By 1940 there would be 400,000 fewer farmers. By the thousands they pulled up stakes and headed to California where they'd heard that people were needed to work the orchards and farms. California produce growers had sent advertisements urging them to come. So off they went – the largest migration of people in American history – the Dust Bowl migration. Families packed everything they had in a Hoover wagon or old truck, tied in the goat or pig, hoisted up their pots and pans, slung on a mattress, and loaded up the kids. "Oakies" and "Arkies" headed west along the "Mother Road" (Route 66) to Cal-i-forn-ai-ay. What they found there was another story! Ridiculed and pushed aside, they also found that the promises of jobs were false. Most were worse off than they had been back home.

Several noteworthy events occurred in the 1930's. The Empire State Building opened in New York City in 1931. The Lindbergh baby was kidnapped and found dead in 1932. In 1933 all banks were closed by President Roosevelt, and the gold standard dropped. Prohibition was repealed in 1933 by the passage of the 21st amendment to the Constitution. The New Deal and Social Security came into being. The first minimum wage law was passed by Congress. Boulder Dam was completed the same year (1936) that *Gone with the Wind* was published. Amelia Earhart was lost in the Pacific, and Orson Welles' radio dramatization of *War of the Worlds* caused a nationwide scare that aliens had landed. The decade ended with the 1939 New York World's Fair and a widening war in Europe.

The teacher can use the information provided in the introduction as a basis for additional short lessons. Scavenger hunts can be held that have small groups of students looking up information about the famous personalities that are listed. Biographical cubes, similar to those in Lesson 8 in the other half of the book, could also be made. The students can roleplay some of the famous people (with appropriate prior research) either for another

class or for "A 20th Century America Time Machine."

It is important that the teacher make liberal use of pictures and films or videos throughout the unit. The students need to see what life what like as well as read about it. Suggestions are included in the Bibliography that will increase students' understanding of immigration, tenement–life, the women's suffrage movement, and the Great Depression.

The ideas in Lesson Plan 1, "20th Century America: The First 40 Years," provide an opportunity to extend an activity begun in one of the other lessons from either *For Better* or *For Worse*. Some of the ideas provide opportunities for other projects or activities that the teacher can assign, make available for choice, or in some other way use to extend the lessons. The lessons within each decade can be reordered to suit the teacher's needs.

In preparation for this part of the unit, the teacher needs to locate magazines, advertisements, music, and other paraphernalia from the twenties and thirties. A tape recording of twenties lingo is desirable in one of the activities. The teacher needs to find and preview films for portions that will be appropriate for each of the decades. The reference librarian at the public library can help locate the names of some. Some video rental stores will assist the teacher as well. The teacher will need a twenties costume and may consider costumes from other decades as well.

Lesson Plan 1

20th Century America: The First 40 Years

OBJECTIVES: To create a tabletop museum that displays realia and books found by the students and examples of the products made by them.

To increase students' understanding of immigration, women's rights in a changing world, the developing problems of the Twenties, and the ghastly after–effects of the Depression — from riding the rails to the Dust Bowl.

MATERIALS: Large tables arranged in groups; reference books on Immigration, Women's Suffrage, World War I, the Plunging Twenties, the Depression, the Stock Market Crash of 1929, Dust Bowl, and any other topics of the time; slides, films or videos, prints (see Bibliography); graphic organizer for recording information from films (example of a Concept Chart provided).*

*Provided at the end of the lesson.

SPECIAL INSTRUCTIONS: The Tabletop Museum includes the projects presented in the book as well as other activities that reflect the life of the early part of this century. An object that is added to the Tabletop Museum might be made in one of the activities in the book. Then students could expand the presentation to include other similar objects that they make. Students may research various items in categories. For example, "Communication and It's Impact on People Then and Now" could include radios, poems, songs, stories, and photography. "Transportation" could include the role of cars, trains, and planes. "Federal Projects and the Reasons for Developing Them" could include FAP and WPA.

It is important that the teacher make liberal use of pictures and films or videos throughout the unit. The students need to see what life what like as well as read about it. Suggestions are included in the Bibliography that will increase students' understanding of immigration, tenement–life, the women's suffrage movement, and the Great Depression.

LENGTH OF TIME: Variable; continuously over the length of the unit.

PROCEDURE:

1. The teacher shows a film or pictures that depict life in the early part of the twentieth century. The students take notes using a graphic organizer (see suggested one at end of lesson).

2. The teacher helps the students to divide themselves into interest areas. Many of the following projects may be built by teams of students.

2. Each group of students collects 10 facts about their area of study and plans how to share this information.

3. Each group completes one of the following projects:

a. Research the history of the camera and its influence on daily life. Collect photographs taken by Jacob A. Riis of immigrant people, sweatshops, and tenements, and make an exhibit. Collect photographs by Walker Evans who documented American life in the 1930's.

b. Make a visual history of your family using documents you can find, birth certificates, photos, artifacts, and old clothing. Go back to the early years of this century if possible.

c. Paint a family tree, starting with you, and going back as far as you can record. (L. Perl. *The Great Ancestor Hunt.* See Bibliography.)

d. Tape an oral history of a family member who remembers the Depression years.

e. Find old sheet music, such as "Brother, Can You Spare A Dime " and learn the song in voice and mime. (P. Seeger, B. Reiser. *Carry It On.* See Bibliography. Also available from Folkways Records as a recording.)

f. Research political cartoons about Women's Suffrage and draw one, taking a pro or con viewpoint. (Jackdaws #P22, *Votes for Women: The Fight for Suffrage.* See Bibliography).

g. Find 10 facts about Ellis Island. Make a maze game of Ellis Island. Include the tunnel leading into Ellis Island, stairways, the Great Hall, and the doctors and inspectors who stopped the immigrants and had the power to send them back.

h. Build a model of the Ford Model T; the Model A; the Hoover Wagon.

i. Find out about traditions and celebrations that immigrants brought to America. Set one up for exhibit. (A. Schwartz. *Cross Your Fingers, Spit in Your Hat* . J.B. Lippincott, 1974).

j. Read C. Aaron's *Lackawanna* (Bibliography) and draw a large map following the childrens' travels as they criss–cross the country.

k. Build a model of the Wright Brothers' plane. (R. Freedman. *The Wright Brothers: How They Invented the Airplane.* Holiday House, 1991).

l. Read J. Hartford's *Steamboat in a Cornfield* (Crown Publ. 1991) and write a rhyme of your own.

m. Read J. Hendershot's *In Coal Country* (Knopf, 1987) and write a poem about your own town. Illustrate with pastel drawings.

n. Photograph members of your family and write short biographies of each member.

o. Build a model or diorama of a General Store, a disappearing part of Americana.

p. Research items which were sold in the 30s. Cut them out of magazines and glue to shelves and counters.

q. Build a radio. (Dorothy and Thomas Hobbler. *And Now , a Word from Our Sponsor.* See Bibliography.)

r. Learn how Wall Street works and invent your own game , "Playing the Market." (M. Bose. *Crash! A New Money Crisis?* New York: Gloucester Press, 1989 and *Cobblestone*, Vol. 7, #4, April 1990, "Taking Stock of Wall Street."

s. Develop the character of Teddy Roosevelt and present yourself at the Tabletop Museum or at "A 20th Century America Time Machine."

t. Plant a WPA table garden (or a garden–in–a–tray).

u. Paint a FAP (Federal Arts Project) mural on a school wall.

v. Research the Jazz Age and ask your music teacher for recordings and tapes. Learn a jazz piece with other members of the band.

After students have made their presentations, the displays are placed in the school library or at a suitable place at "A 20th Century America Time Machine" program. It may be possible to set up a lending library of books, toys, games, models, or other tabletop items and realia.

Concept Chart

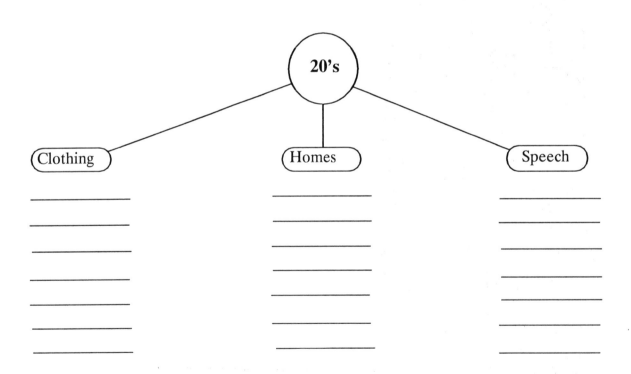

20TH CENTURY AMERICA
FOR WORSE

The Plunging Twenties

Lesson Plan 2

The 20's Vocabulary

OBJECTIVES: To learn 20's vocabulary words for "A 20th Century America Time Machine."

To compare and analyze 20's words with jargon used by young people today.

MATERIALS: "The 20's Vocabulary List,"* blackboard (See TIME/LIFE's *This Fabulous Century 1920-1930*, for a more complete listing of vocabulary.); teacher costume; Concept Chart (see example in Lesson 1).

SPECIAL INSTRUCTIONS: The teacher needs to prepare a short speech that is full of expressions from the twenties. An example is given in the procedure part of the lesson. If the teacher is able to acquire a tape recording of someone speaking in the vocabulary of the twenties, it will increase the students' ability to hold conversations. A excerpt from one of the movies (or videos) listed in the Bibliography needs to be shown.

The teacher needs to construct a costume that is reminiscent of the period and wear it for this lesson. Men could wear suits with a cane and hat and maybe a fur coat; women could wear knee–length dresses with a belted and dropped waistline and hat and gloves similar to those shown in the illustration, "Dressing for the Twenties" with Lesson 3. The same costume is worn for the third lesson as well.

LENGTH OF TIME: 45 minutes.

PROCEDURE:

1. The teacher enters the class dressed in a costume reminiscent of the twenties and introduces the lesson with a previously prepared script that incorporates several expressions from the twenties. An example is as follows:

> At the risk of being a *flat tire* I left my *cheaters* at home, pulled on my duds and look like a *flapper* or a *cake–eater*. It's the *bee's knees*, real *hotsy-totsy*! Hope it's *jake* by you!

2. The teacher asks the students to identify the expressions that he or she used that are unfamiliar. They make an educated guess as to what they may mean. The teacher then distributes the "20's Vocabulary List," and the students compare their guesses with the definitions.

3. The class lists all the expressions on the vocabulary list that they have heard used before. They identify any that have meanings to them that are different from those listed.

4. The teacher asks the students for a definition of slang and aks them to name any slang expressiosns that they use. The teacher lists these expressions on the blackboard. Class discusses where these words may have originated from. (Are they rap music phrases, shortened forms of other words, or used by people they look up to?)

5. The class writes down these 90's expressions and writes mutually–agreed–upon definitions to these words. They tell how these words represent their culture and postulate as to which of them will become part of our vocabulary, which are just a fad, and how long these words will last and why.

6. The class looks at the twenties vocabulary list again and decides if they are able to update any of the expressions into nineties lingo.

7. The teacher asks the class if other periods of time had other words and expressions that they used and continues the discussion with questions like the following:

   a. Why would a generation of young people develop their own form of communication?

   b. What does language do for a group?

   c. Are rebellious youth unique to the 1920's?

8. The class prepares for the parts they will play in the "Algonquin Round Table" discussion by writing a short story in which at least 10 of these expressions are used.

9. Students practice using these expressions in conversation.

10. The expressions are also used in the "Plunging Twenties" portion of "A 20th Century America Time Machine" program.

Fact Sheet

The 20's Vocabulary

Something phenomenal occurred in the language of young people during the 1920's. It happened as the result of the desire by rebellious youths to defy the established customs of their parents. It was a harmless rebellion, and it took the country by storm, much to the annoyance of parents. The following list gives an excellent view of life through the words of the flapper. It also shows us how words work their way into our culture as many of these terms remain in our everyday speech.

ALL WET: wrong, as in "He's all wet."

BALONEY: a derogatory term such as "No way!" or "That's a bunch of baloney."

BEE'S KNEES: superb person, such as "She's the bee's knees."

BELLY LAUGH: a loud, uninhibited laugh.

BLIND DATE: a date with someone you don't know, usually arranged by friends.

BIG CHEESE: an important person.

BULL SESSION: an informal group discussion.

BUMP OFF: to murder.

BUNK: ridiculous, as in "That's a lot of bunk."

CAKE–EATER: a ladies' man.

CARRY A TORCH: to love someone, and not be loved back.

CAT'S MEOW OR CAT'S PAJAMAS: the best.

CHEATERS: eyeglasses.

COPACETIC (co–pa–SET–ic): excellent.

CRUSH: being enchanted with someone, as "She has a crush on her teacher."

DOGS: human feet, as "My dogs are tired tonight."

FLAPPER: a 20's girl with bobbed hair, short skirt, and rolled stockings.

FLAT TIRE: a boring person, a nerd.

FRAME: to get someone in trouble by giving false statements, as in "He framed me. I didn't do it."

GAMS: girls' legs, as in "She's got a nice–looking pair of gams."

GATECRASHER: someone who comes to a party uninvited.

GOOFY: silly, as in "He's too, too goofy."

GYP: to cheat, as in "She gyped me out of the lunch she promised."

HARD–BOILED: unsentimental, tough, as in "What a hard–boiled character he is!"

HEEBIE–JEEBIES: the willies, the jitters, as "You give me the heebie–jeebies when you talk like that."

HEP: wise, as in "I'm hep to that."

HOTSY–TOTSY: pleasing.

JAKE: O.K.; as in "That's jake by me."

JALOPY: an old car.

KIDDO: addressing someone you know, like "Hey, kiddo."

KISSER: the mouth, as in "Pow, right in the kisser."

LOUSY: bad, as in "What a lousy day it is."

PINCH: to arrest, as in "Watch out that you don't get pinched."

PUSHOVER: a person who is easily influenced, as in "He's a pushover."

RUN–AROUND: delaying a response, as in "She's giving me the run–around."

SCRAM: to leave hurridly, as in "I'd better scram outta here."

SHEBA: a good–looking woman.

SHEIK: a good–looking man.

SPIFFY: sharply dressed, "Boy, do you look spiffy."

STUCK ON: having a crush on, as in "He's stuck on her."

SWELL: (noun) a sophisticated person, as in "He's a swell from Manhattan."; (verb) marvelous, as in "That's swell."

UPCHUCK: to vomit.

WHOOPIE: a great time, as in "We made whoopie last night."

Lesson Plan 3
Dressing For The Twenties

OBJECTIVES: To build costumes to be worn, as a famous character, at "A 20th Century America Time Machine" or at the "Algonquin Round Table," Lesson Plan 3.
To research costumes of the 1920's.
To research famous people to roleplay in "A 20th Century America Time Machine."

MATERIALS: Articles of clothing from home; "Dressing For The Twenties Illustration";* "Dressing for the Twenties: Boys/Girls;"* excerpts from film such as *The Little Rascals* (1994, based on *Our Gang* short films of 1922–1944) or *Bugsy Malone* with Jodie Foster and an all–child cast (1976, a spoof on gangster movies, available on video); replicas of ads placed on wall of room; old magazines from 1920's (*Saturday Evening Post* with its Norman Rockwell covers, *Literary Digest*, *Farm Journal* or similar magazines.); teacher costume from Lesson 2; Concept Chart (see example in Lesson 1).
*Provided at the end of the lesson.

SPECIAL INSTRUCTIONS: The Concept Chart is an integral part of the notetaking for each of the decades. It helps to organize the information for comparison and contrast of the decades with today' lifestyles.

LENGTH OF TIME: 30–45 minutes on two different days plus time at home.

PROCEDURE:

1. The teacher greets the students in an outfit that has an early 20th century look to it. The teacher has students look through old magazines or at the ads that have been placed on the wall. After a few moments the teacher stops and asks the class questions like the following:

   a.   What can you tell about the characterization I am representing from what you have just seen?

   b.   How is my clothing like that that I usually wear? How is it different?

   c.   Has anyone seen the recently released *The Little Rascals* movie? Are there any similarities in the clothing?

   d.   Do you suppose men always wore suits? Did women always wear gloves and a hat?

2. The teacher shows part of a film or video. The students use their Concept Chart to record information as they find it. They can use another Concept Chart for the nineties, which will allow comparison and contrast with today.

3. The teacher passes out the illustrations of clothing from the twenties. Students add to their Concept Charts any similarities and differences in the clothing of the twenties from

that worn today.

4. The students discuss how clothing from home can be used to create clothing reminiscent of the twenties. Students write their ideas down and take them home. For example, boys' clothing consisted of a suit or a pair of "baggies" pushed up to the knees and tied ("plus fours"). The latter were worn with a pair of argyle socks or printed kneesocks. (Warning—no cute cartoon characters here.) "Spats," worn with the suit, can be made by cutting a pair of white athletic socks, as illustrated, and worn over a pair of shoes.

5. Girls' dresses (trousers weren't yet in the picture—first coming into fashion in the 30's and then only in the cities) are worn loose, because it was a statement of women's new freedom. The girls can try on mother's dress, or choose a simple long nightgown and tie it around the hips with a long, wide sash. The dress should be pulled up to the knees and allowed to blouse over the sash. Women wore lots and lots of long costume jewelry, especially strings of pearls or beads. The girls can make large crepe paper or tissue flowers of coordinating colors to attach to their shoulders, hips, and shoes. A flower can even be added to a snug hat. (Ski caps work very well if an old felt hat is unavailable.) A colorful headband can be worn around the forehead.

6. Since fur, especially raccoon, was very popular in the twenties, both boys and girls might top off their outfits with an old fur coat or a fake fur. A long, simple, huge fur coat can be made using fake fur cloth purchased at any fabric store. The bigger, the better. Props may include a golf club or cane, or a college banner, which was taken to football games.

7. The students collect clothing from home and bring it to class.

8. The students mix and match clothing with each other to assemble a complete costume.

9. When students have decided on a costume, a costume party can be staged, or the students can form a parade and visit other classrooms.

DRESSING FOR THE TWENTIES · YOU'LL NEED: BOYS

"plus fours" and argyle socks

a hat

golf club or cane

"spats"

2 or 3 pc. suit

1920 - 1930

YOU'LL NEED: GIRLS

large flowers (paper, silk)

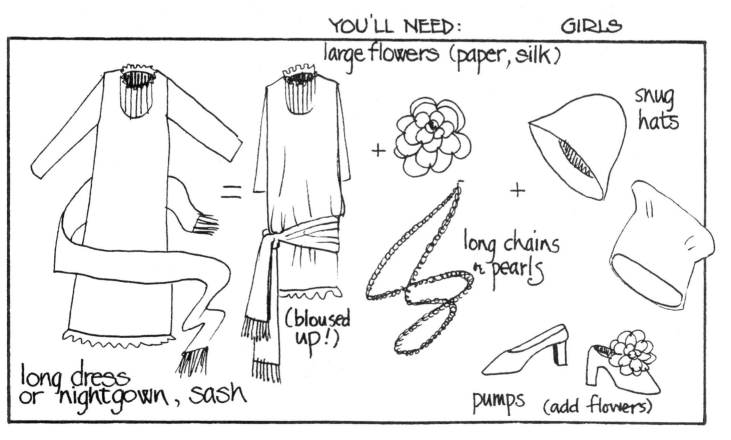

snug hats

+

long chains n' pearls

+

(bloused up!)

long dress or nightgown, sash

pumps (add flowers)

Lesson Plan 4

The Algonquin Round Table

OBJECTIVES: To roleplay a Round Table discussion.

To become familiar with quips and quotes from original members, choose a particular character of the Round Table, and perform a dramatic piece for "A 20th Century America Time Machine."

MATERIALS: Costumes (see Lesson 2); fact sheet, "Algonquin Round Table;"* books such as Robert E. Drennan, Ed. *The Algonquin Wits* ; J. Bryan III. *Merry Gentlemen (And One Lady)*; *Bartlett's Familiar Quotations*; James R. Gaines. *Wit's End: Days and Nights of the Algonquin Round Table*. (See Bibliography.); (optional) video camera; excerpts (see Bibliography) from any Marx Brothers video; *Top Hat* (Fred Astaire and Ginger Rogers, 1935); *Swing High, Swing Low*, (Carole Lombard and Fred MacMurray, 1937); *Dinner at Eight* (John and Lionel Barrymore, Wallace Beery, Marie Dressler, and Jean Harlow, 1933); or *Mrs. Parker and the Vicious Circle* (Jennifer Jason Leigh and Campbell Scott, 1994).

SPECIAL INSTRUCTIONS: The teacher needs to preview any of the films or videos available to the class and select portions to show that illustrate the use of puns and other verbal characterizations. An excerpt from a video of a Bob Hope, Red Skelton, or Marx Brothers film could be used to illustrate whether jokes are funny or not. This activity is best with sixth through eighth grade students (or older), but portions of it may be appropriate for some elementary students.

LENGTH OF TIME: 2 one–hour preparation periods, 30 minute performance.

PROCEDURE:

1. The teacher tells a joke from the past that the students wouldn't understand and waits for the students to laugh. An example can be taken from the fact sheet. Then the teacher tells another joke that is current, at which they will laugh. Alternatively, the teacher can show an excerpt from an older movie or ask the students to tell a joke that they think is funny. The teacher then asks questions like the following:

   a. What is the difference between the jokes? Why is one funny and the other not?

   b. What are the characteristics of a good joke? (Answer: Person hearing the joke must understand the words and the inferences of the words; if they relate to something in the news the person must be familiar with it.)

2. The teacher then asks the students the meaning of a pun. (Answer: a pun is a play on meaning or sound of words that is funny). The class tries to think of puns with which they are familiar.

3. The students are asked to define and illustrate the word, sarcasm. (Answer: a caustic remark that is frequently ironic—means the opposite from what is actually said.) Example: "That's a real good job you just did," said in a sarcastic, belittling manner that implies it's a terrible job.

4. If possible, the teacher shows the class selected portions of one of the videos or films listed in the materials section. The class is told that during the twenties a group of friends who were just starting to make their way in the literary or theatrical fields used to meet for lunch at the Algonquin Hotel in New York City. They would end up telling each other jokes, each one trying to best or even insult the other, all the while remaining the best of friends.

5. The teacher lists the names of several of the people who frequented the Algonquin Hotel on the blackboard. The students either select or are assigned a name to research either in an encyclopedia, biographical dictionary, or one of the resources included in the materials section. Ten or more facts should be found about each individual.

6. The fact sheet is distributed and read. The teacher asks questions like the following:

    a.   Why would people do this sort of thing? Were they angry at each other?

    b.   Do you and your friends ever say things about each other and still remain friends?

    c.   What is the difference between the way the members of the Algonquin Round Table spoke to each other and the way you and your friends may speak to each other when you are angry?

7. Using the resource books above, students find 5 quotations spoken or written by the character they selected or were assigned. The quotes need to be memorized.

8. In small groups, the students recite the quotes to each other. They discuss the meaning of the quotes and what they have in common.

9. Each small Round Table group of students tries to tie the quotes together into a short skit. They discuss how their quotes might work into a creative dramatic piece that can be loosely tied together by the quotes.

For example, the following quotes might have been gathered:

"I haven't been abroad for so long that I almost speak English without an accent."— Benchley.

"This year I've done two things I wanted to do—go to Peking and act in a play. Next year I want to go to Russia and try umbrella mending."—Woollcott.

"I can think of 40 better places to spend the summer, all of them on Long Island in a hammock."—Harpo Marx.

"Being an old maid is like death by drowning, a really delightful sensation after you cease to struggle." —Edna Ferber.

"You can't take it with you."—George C. Kaufmann.

"Stop looking at the world through rose-colored bifocals."—Dorothy Parker.

"Men seldom make passes at girls who wear glasses." — Dorothy Parker.

"When I was born I owed twelve dollars." — George C. Kaufmann.

"There is less in this than meets the eye." — Tallulah Bankhead.

10. The students study their quotations and decide if there is a theme or natural movement from one idea to another. The Round Table group plans a skit around a theme, perhaps each person musing about his or her life or travels. They flesh out the quotes by introducing more dialogue. Examples are as follows:

Kaufmann: "When I was born I owed twelve dollars."

Bankhead: "Running up bills at such a young age? There's less in this than meets the eye."

11. Each Round Table group of students writes a short script and rehearses the banter going back and forth across the table. They should use plenty of arm and body motions. For example, Woollcott might stand and strut while speaking his lines, while Dorothy Parker sits back, tilts back her head, and delivers her lines without cracking a smile. Gestures and facial expressions are very important to keep the audience interested. (If the movie, *Mrs. Parker and the Vicious Circle*, is available the students should observe portions of it at this time.)

12. The students continue to research their characters, picking out one feature that is individual to that character. For example, Dorothy Parker was rather dowdy and favored embroidered peasant outfits; George C. Kaufman was a nervous man and very shy; and Alexander Woollcott was large and noisy and loved to eat.

13. The students practice with 3–4 run–throughs and tighten the interpretation of the dramatic piece for performing in front of other classrooms or at "A 20th Century America Time Machine" presentation. The performance can be videotaped and shown later.

14. The students individually write about this experience and what each learned from it. Questions like the following should be included in what is written:

a. What do you think of the Algonquin group?

b. Can you think of any current group of people who might be as influential as this group was? Why or why not?

15. The Algonquin Round Table group had a favorite word game that members continually played with each other. Called "I–Can–Give–You–A–Sentence," it involved a sentence in which one person used a multi–syllabic word that sounded like an unrelated phrase. For example, "I know a farmer who has two daughters, Lizzie and Tillie. Lizzie is all right, but you have no idea how punctilious." (punk Tillie is) — George S. Kaufmann (*The Algonquin Wits*). If the class has a high level of interest and vocabulary development, they might like to try this game. The students need to list some vocabulary words that have three or more syllables and try to make sentences that change the words into phrases. Playing the word game, Hinky Pinky or Hinkedy Pinkedy, is helpful.

The Algonquin Round Table

In 1920 Frank Case, owner of the Algonquin Hotel in New York City reserved a round table in the Rose Room to accommodate a group of people who often gathered to have lunch, match wits, and throw out good natured insults to one another. They were the intelligentia—the highbrows—who during the twenties and thirties set the climate for what was happening in American literature and theater. The Round Table was what was happening, and envious bystanders longed to be part of that select few. But it wasn't a club. Rather, this group of brilliant humorists and wags shared a common irreverence—even to calling themselves the "Vicious Circle." Their mutual interests were literary and theatrical. They didn't take themselves too seriously, treating every possible subject with some degree of humor. They were outrageous, articulate, gregarious, and the toast of the town. Lunches lasted for hours and were feasts of mind, food, great talk, and polka (a card game).

Though the Round Table group started out as unknowns, they achieved fame through their magazine articles, reviews, and stage and screen productions and performances. The usual group numbered about 20, though others came and went over the years. Three members of the *Vanity Fair* (magazine) writing staff who were fast friends—Dorothy Parker, Robert Benchley, and Robert Sherwood—started the whole thing, and others soon joined them.

The puns and barbs of this group became part of the American language. Benchley said, "A dog teaches a boy fidelity, perseverance, and to turn around three times before lying down." Another delightful story attributed to Benchley tells of the time he was coming out of a New York restaurant and needed a cab. He saw a uniformed man at the restaurant door and asked, "Would you get us a taxi, please." The man answered coldly, "I'm sorry. I happen to be a rear admiral in the United States Navy." "All right, then," said Benchley, "get us a battleship." It was comments such as these and "Let's get out of wet clothes and into a dry martini" that have brought chuckles for 60 years.

By the end of the twenties, the Great Depression put a strangle hold on humor. America didn't feel much like laughing. George S. Kaufman summed it up by stating, "Comedy has become like castor oil. People fight it." The Round Table lived on, but it wasn't quite the same. Other members of the old guard included:

Heywood Braun	George S. Kaufman	Ring Lardner	Harold Ross
Alexander Woollcott	Edna Ferber	Marc Connelly	Frank Sullivan
Harpo Marx	Herman Mankiewicz	Irvin S. Cobb	Peggy Wood
Charles MacArthur	Frank Crowninshield	Tallulah Bankhead	Paul Robeson
Beatrice Kaufman	Alice Duer Miller	Irving Berlin	Joyce Barbour
Herbert Baynard Swope		Franklin Pierce Adams (called FPA by his friends)	

Lesson Plan 5

Jazz: Call–and–Response in 20's Lingo

OBJECTIVES:	To understand the somewhat complicated rhythm pattern of jazz. To perform a call and response activity for "A 20th Century America Time Machine."
MATERIALS:	Fact sheet, "Call and Response in 20's Lingo;"* jazz music selections. *Provided at the end of the lesson.
SPECIAL INSTRUCTIONS:	The teacher can ask the music teacher to introduce some jazz pieces to the students. They listen to the rhythms and clap out the beats.
LENGTH OF TIME:	20–30 minutes.

PROCEDURE:

1. The teacher or music teacher introduces some jazz pieces to the students. The teacher distributes the fact sheet, and the students read it. The teacher then asks the students questions like the following:

    a. How is the jazz music you heard different from the music to which you usually listen?

    b. Are there any similarities?

    c. How might rap music be similar to the chants of the West Africans who were brought to this country as slaves?

    d. Why did it take so long for jazz to become popular in most parts of the country?

    e. Is rap music understood by the majority of the people in this country? Why or why not? Can you see similarities between rap music and the music of the twenties?

2. The teacher explains that the students can best understand the rhythm of jazz by practicing a chant that is like a call–and–response song. The class forms a circle. Each student calls off a number and remembers it.

3. The chant, beginning with student #1.

    #1: Number 5 is a swell and a gate crasher.

    #5: Who, me?

    #1: I'm hep.

    #5: Couldn't be

    #1: You bet.

    #5: Number 11 is a swell and a gate crasher.

The same chant continues, back and forth, across the circle until all have participated.

4. The students clap with the beat. They may vary the claps, as illustrated below:

Four claps per measure are used without the grace note; five claps per measure are used with the grace note.

ONE–two–three–four; ONE–two–three–four

uh–ONE–two–three–four; uh–ONE–two–three–four

(The "uh" is the grace note.)

5. The students practice and perform this call–and–response song at "A 20th Century America Time Machine" program.

Fact Sheet

Call–and–Response in 20's Lingo

Jazz had its beginnings in West African music that African slaves brought to this country. Africans used music all the time—for planting and harvesting, in ceremonies, during preparations for battle. Music was part of their daily life. As slaves in this country they used music to communicate and send messages, to tell about the Underground Railroad, and to ease their everyday drudgery. The rhythm of their music was interpretive and improvisational. One drummer might play a steady 1–2–1–2 rhythm and another played a steady 1–2–3 rhythm. Another drummer might add his third rhythm. Then they combined it all.

Jazz combines African music with songs and music of the slaves, ragtime (hesitant, jerky rhythms which were known as "ragged time" and shortened to "ragtime"), and blues (music to ease the sadness and "blues" of slaves).

By the late nineteenth century jazz had made New Orleans the the music center of America. It had infused the life of a whole array of people—Spanish, French, Creole, and Indian, as well as blacks. Some of the era's famous black musicians and singers were Eubie Blake, Louis Armstrong, Bessie Smith, Ma Rainey, and Jelly Roll Morton. By 1920 a great many dancehalls and saloons closed because of the Prohibition Amendment, and musicians found themselves out of work. (The 18th amendment to the Constitution, ratified in 1918, ordered that the manufacture, sale, and transportation of intoxicating liquor was prohibited.) Many of the musicians went north, and jazz moved from New Orleans into America's mainstream. Chicago took over as the jazz capital of the country.

DOING THE CHARLESTON

Lesson Plan 6

Doin' the Charleston

OBJECTIVES: To learn the Charleston, a dance of the 20s.

To perform the Charleston at "A 20th Century America Time Machine."

MATERIALS: Illustration, "The Charleston".*

*Provided at the end of the lesson.

SPECIAL INSTRUCTIONS: During the 1920's the Charleston was an extremely popular jazz dance. It could be danced alone or with a group. The Charleston was known by its peculiar toes–in, heels–out steps. Originally a black folk dance from West Africa where dancers swirled in wild abandon, it regained popularity in a more sedate manner near Charleston, South Carolina. In 1923, after its introduction in the black musical, *Runnin' Wild*, it became a national phenomenon. This activity uses a basic Charleston step, which is varied with forward and backward kicks and different arm movements. The teacher can ask the music teacher for recorded Charleston music, which is in quick 4/4 time and uses a syncopated rhythm. Teachers may be able to demonstrate the Charleston steps or find someone who can, thereby permitting students to learn the steps in less time.

LENGTH OF TIME: 45 minutes.

PROCEDURE:

1. The teacher asks the students to name the dances with which they are familiar. He or she can add to the student's list. Students research the dates when each of these dances was the most popular. This research will help them to see that dances come in and out of popularity the same way that music does. The teacher asks the class if anyone has heard of the Charleston and explains that that was one of the dances that was popular during the twenties.

2. The students learn to dance the Charleston by starting with simple steps and gradually increasing their complexity. They refer to the illustration, "The Charleston."

Step I—Point toes inward, knees together. At the count of 1, bend knees; Count 2, stand straight; Count 3, bend knees; Count 4, stand straight. Repeat in 4/4 time, until class is working in unison. Bring elbows up at the 1 and 3 count, as illustrated in Step I.

Step II—Continue bending knees at 1 and 3 count. Kick right leg up, toe in, at 1 and 3 count. Elbows up, at 1 and 3 count.

Step III—Vary kicks, as illustrated. Count 1, right leg forward; Count 3, left leg forward. As students become familiar and comfortable with these basic movements, they might kick sideways, kick backwards, or sway their bodies. The weight is shifted from one leg to another. Students try forward and backward kicks as they move forward. As the students become better they can swing their arms.

3. The students prepare a Charleston dance for sharing with other classes or for "A 20th Century Time Machine" program.

THE CHARLESTON

Lesson Plan 7

Get Rich Overnight!

OBJECTIVES: To learn about the stock market and how it works.

To simulate the experiences of some investors who bought on margin in the twenties.

MATERIALS: Fact sheet, "Wall Street";* fact sheet, "Stock Market Crash of 1929";* "Promissory Note."*
*Provided at the end of the lesson.

SPECIAL INSTRUCTIONS: The teacher must adopt the mannerisms of a "con man" in this simulation and ham–up the introduction. It is helpful to set the stage with one or two of the students beforehand and make sure they will go along with the gag. The students selected should be popular members of the class, ones that others look up to. One of these students is given a dollar to use in the simulation. The teacher also has another teacher or other adult primed to enter the room at a signal and take the money for investment. The same teacher comes back ten minutes before the end of the period and hands him or her a note about a phone message that has been received. Using at least some real money increases the interest in the simulation. (For example, the teacher can show a stack of bills with a twenty on the top and bottom, the rest being fake money.) The lent money does not have to be shown, but the dollar that the first student invests must be real. If the teacher is uncomfortable in pulling off this gag, it is possible that an older students would be successful. In that case the teacher can be the first one to give money for investment.

LENGTH OF TIME: One hour or more; must be completed in one class period.

PROCEDURE:

1. In a conspiratorial tone, the teacher tells the class that he or she learned a hot tip in the stock market the night before. It seems that an American company that makes chocolate cookies is about to be taken over by a well–known European company. The teacher only knows about this situation because the person he or she spoke to is a first cousin of the vice–president of the European company. It's very hush–hush, but he or she has already invested in this company and hopes to make a lot of money fast. The students could participate in this investment with him or her to a limited extent, but it must be done before the end of the class period. (The opportunity to change a dollar into two dollars overnight must be made enticingly clear to the students.) The teacher has already invested one thousand dollars. Do any of the students want to invest five or ten dollars?

2. One of the students to whom the teacher has previously talked looks through his or her pocket and finds a dollar and offers it to the teacher for investment. The teacher tells the student that it is an insufficent amount, but that he or she will lend the student four dollars so that the investment can be made. The stock sells for five dollars per share. The

interest the student owes the teacher will be only twenty–five cents per day per dollar. That means that by this time tomorrow the student will be able to pay back the teacher and still have money left over. The teacher asks the class to calculate how much each of them would have and how much each of them would owe the teacher when the stock doubles by tomorrow if they have each invested five dollars. If any students want to invest but don't have the money, they can borrow from the teacher. The teacher tells them this practice is called "buying on margin" and is completely legal. The students must understand that normally he or she would lend the money to them at lower rates, but since the money he or she is lending is money that could be invested and doubled, the rate has to be twenty–five cents on the dollar. The second student to whom the teacher has spoken now decides to invest five dollars, even though he or she has no money at all and must borrow it all. This student says, "I want to invest five dollars, but I will need to borrow it all from you. But that sounds o.k. to me, because by this time tomorrow I'll have ten dollars and only owe you a dollar and a quarter plus the five dollars you lent me. So I will have made three dollars and seventy-five cents even though I didn't have any money at the start."

3. The teacher lends all the money that he or she can and has the students each sign a Promissory Note. Many students who would otherwise not participate in such a venture may do so when the pressure from other students builds up. The teacher adds to the enthusiasm to buy by telling the students that the stock price of the Chocolate Cooky Company has been rising consistently. Last week alone the person the teacher met made almost five hundred dollars on money he invested. At this point another teacher or other adult (with whom the teacher has made prearrangements) enters the room and takes the money to the office where the first cousin of the vice–president of the European company is waiting.

4. The teacher tells the class that, since they have become investors in the stock market, they need to learn more about it. The fact sheet, "Wall Street," is distributed and read. If any students express concern about their money, the teacher allays their fears. Talk should continue about how much money they are all going to make.

5. Approximately ten minutes before the end of class the other teacher or adult returns to the room with a sad face and a written message from the cousin of the vice president of the European company. The teacher reads it to the class with much melodrama. The note should say something like the following:

Dear _____,

I invested your money and that of your students in the chocolate cookie company as you requested. The price was five dollars per share. Unfortunately the bottom seems to have fallen out of the market and the price of the shares of the company has declined to $3.50. In addition, the margin is being called so all of you must come up with the money you owe within the hour or lose your stock.

The teacher expresses horror and tells the students that they will have to pay her or him

back immediately as the price is dropping and the teacher can not afford to lose all that money. If they cannot pay, they will need to give the teacher something else of value that they possess.

6. At this point the teacher needs to start debriefing the students. They are told, if they don't already realize it, that the whole scenario was fictional. It did, however, simulate what happened to many people at the time of the crash on Wall Street. People were left owing money they had no way of getting. Some lost everything they had including their homes. The teacher asks questions like the following:

    a. What was the problem that we dealt with in the simulation?

    b. At what point did you begin to be concerned about your money?

    c. Why did you invest your money?

    d. Did you find the idea of getting rich quickly appealing?

7. The teacher distributes the fact sheet, "Stock Market Crash of 1929," and the students read it. The teacher asks additional questions like the following:

    a. What happened to companies and shareholders who continued to hold their stock when the prices started down?

    b. What happened to the banks that lent people the money to invest?

    c. When no one had enough money what would happen to other businesses like automobile production, clothing manufacture, and even agriculture?

    d. What would have happened if you lived at that time but never speculated or even bought any stock?

Promissory Note

I, the undersigned, promise to repay _____

the sum of _____ together with the interest thereon at the rate of

twenty–five cents per day for a total amount of _____, which sum

shall be payable upon demand in its entirety.

Signed this _____th day of _____, 19__.

_____

Signature of Borrower

_____

Signature of Lender

Wall Street

Wall Street, New York City, is a major financial center. It is here that stocks and bonds are traded, bought, and sold. Since we now live in a global market stock exchanges today are also in Tokyo, London, and other cities around the world. In the 20's and 30's the stock market was a little less complicated. Back then Americans felt the immense pride of "owning their share of American business." Today people are more apt to own shares in a mutual fund that owns a lot of different companies; in the twenties people usually became shareholders of companies or corporations directly through buying stocks in these companies. They felt it was the American dream to be part of a company. By investing in a company, they financed improvements, gave jobs to more people, developed more products or equipment that helped our economy grow.

In order to get start–up money, you need INVESTORS who are willing to give you money for your business venture. You must have ASSETS and WORKING CAPITAL. To get investors you must give up some of your ownership. This means that you must divide your business into pieces. You form a CORPORATION, with a BOARD OF DIRECTORS. The Board of Directors issues SHARES of STOCK for you and your investors. Because you developed the product and are responsible for producing it, you hold the most stock (over 50%).

Assets: Property, material, and equipment owned by (in this case) the entrepreneur (person who started the business).

Board of Directors: A group of people who control the affairs of a business enterprise.

Capital: Money or property owned or used in business by a person, partnership, or corporation. WORKING capital is money used to start up a business.

Corporation: A group of people that legally has its own rights, privileges, and liabilities separate from those of each of its members.

Shares: Capital stock of a company that is divided into equal parts for shareholders.

Stock: The capital a company raises through selling shares that allow the shareholder to own a part of the company.

Fact Sheet

Stock Market Crash of 1929

Come on! Jump on the stock market band wagon! What fun! Instant money and instant success! People from all walks of life were playing the stock market—housewives, shopgirls, elevator operators, laborers, business men, bankers. They bought shares in companies. Companies used the money to improve their operations, making more money. During the 20's people bought on speculation, buying stocks because they expected the stock values to go up when they could sell them for much higher prices. As stocks rose higher and higher, shareholders borrowed money from banks to buy more. They could sell high, repay bank debts, and still make a nice profit.

What was happening? By 1929 stock prices were higher than the company's worth. Who wanted to pay so high a price for these stocks? Sell 'em! Fast! And that's what started the CRASH. Sellers rushed to get rid of their stocks, but there were few buyers. Stocks started to drop in value, thundering down and down. The stock market lost over fifty billion dollars between 1929 and 1931.

Black Thursday, (October 29, 1929) was the beginning of the Great Depression. Who it affected, what it did, and how long it lasted may be explored in the next section of this book, "The Depressed Thirties."

20ᵀᴴ CENTURY AMERICA
FOR WORSE

The Depressed Thirties

Lesson Plan 8
"Brother, Can You Spare a Dime?"

OBJECTIVES: To learn a song that summarizes the disillusion and pain of those who felt pushed aside and forgotten.

To sing this song at "A 20th Century America Time Machine" program.

MATERIALS: Sheet music, "Brother, Can You Spare a Dime?";* fact sheet, "Brother, Can You Spare a Dime?";* Milton Meltzer. *Brother, Can You Spare a Dime?* (see Bibliography); (optional) video or film showing a newsreel from the thirties that showed the strikes (Many resource centers have these newsreels arranged by decades. Several publishers have done it. As an alternative, the teacher shows pictures from one of the Time/Life books.); (optional) Pete Seeger and Bob Reiser. *Carry It Off* (See Bibliography.).

*Provided at the end of the lesson.

LENGTH OF TIME: 45 minutes.

PROCEDURE:

1. If available, the teacher introduces the strikes and marches of the thirties by showing part of a newsreel from that time, either a video or movie. Alternatively, pictures of the times from various books can be shown. Students discuss the word, *protest*, and what it means. They list some protest marches that have happened in recent times, decide if they brought about change, and if so, how.

2. The teacher distributes the fact sheet on the song, "Brother, Can You Spare a Dime?" and the students read it.

3. The teacher reads the class Chapter 13 in Milton Meltzer's book, *Brother, Can You Spare a Dime?* It describes the demonstrations, marches, and walk on Washington by the Bonus Army. The teacher leads a discussion of the time by asking questions like the following:

   a. What is the difference between revolution and evolution.?

   b. Which of these methods of change took place in the thirties?

   c. What was the outcome of the changes? Did it improve the conditions of most people in the country or not?

4. The teacher asks the students to read the song together in unison and asks questions like the following:

   a. What do you think is meant by "Say, don't you remember, they called me Al, it was Al all the time. . . say, don't you remember, I'm your pal." — then "Buddy, can you spare a dime?"

   b. What is the meaning of the phrase, "falling through the cracks in the system."

5. The students learn the lyrics and the music of the song and sing it with feeling. They practice it for inclusion at "A 20th Century America Time Machine" program.

6. As an optional additional activity, the class can complete one or more of the following ideas, either for the Tabletop Museum or for "A 20th Century America Time Machine" program:

   a. The teacher tells the students that Pete Seeger and Bob Reiser have written a book, *Carry It Off,* which is about American working people and the songs about them. Chapter 4 covers union songs and ballads about poverty. It includes songs like "Hurry, Hurry, Hurry," sung to the tune of "John Brown's Body" that starts out with the line, "Mine eyes have seen the glory of the making of a Ford." Mass production was rushing on. The students can take a well–known tune and write their own lyrics that tell a story about their own time and its problems. Suggestions would be the environment, world events, or town events.

   b. "The Soup Song" sung to the tune of "My Bonnie Lies Over the Ocean" in the same book tells about flophouse living and days spent on the street. The teacher directs students' attention to one of today's problems — homelessness — and asks students what the present–day equivalent of flophouses are. The students briefly discuss whether homeless shelters are the final answer to anything. Students can write a soup kitchen or homeless shelter song to a familiar tune, which can be recorded or sung at "A 20th Century America Time Machine" program.

   c. "I Don't Want Your Millions, Mister" is a song about not needing lots of money — just enough for "food for the babies and my old job back." The teacher leads a brief discussion of the present–day economy and joblessness in America. The students tell if they know of anyone who has been laid off from his or her job, or who can't find work? They discuss what it must be like to cut back on extras and spend money only on the necessities. The class can identify some of the safety nets available today that were not there for people in the thirties.

BROTHER, CAN YOU SPARE A DIME?

© 1932

Words by E. Y HARBURG
Music by JAY GORNEY

With much expression

In strict tempo

Once I built a rail - road, Once I built a tow - er, Made it run,— made it race— a - gainst time.
Once I built a rail - road, Once I built a tow - er, to the sun,— Brick and ri - vet and lime.

Now it's done,— Broth - er, Can You Spare A Dime?

Once in kha - ki suits, Gee, we looked swell Full of that Yan - kee Doo - dle - de - dum.

Half a mil - lion boots went slog - gin' thru Hell, I was the kid— with the drum.—

Say don't you re - mem - ber, they called me "Al," It was "Al" all the time,

Say, don't you re - mem - ber I'm your Pal— Bud - dy, Can You Spare A Dime?

WITH PERMISSION FROM WARNER BROS. PUBL. INC.

Song: "Brother, Can You Spare a Dime?"

America was hurting. Disillusioned and feeling an overwhelming sense of hopelessness, people struggled to survive in their daily battle to find work, to feed their children, and to keep a roof over their heads. They staged hunger strikes to keep from going hungry and participated in riots over a loaf of bread.

After the war the U.S. Government passed the Patman Bill (1924) that promised war bonuses to veterans to be paid in 1945. As the Depression deepened, veterans first asked, then demanded, to have their money now. Though President Hoover refused, Congress overrode his decision and paid out half the money. In 1932 a large straggly group of veterans marched on Washington to demand the rest. This "Bonus Army," 20,000 strong, hunkered down in make–shift tents and cardboard boxes. After several bouts with government tanks and guns, they disbanded, and with low spirits, left the city.

Patriotism? They had defended their country. They had come to Washington to protest the holding back of money rightfully owed them. They had worked as civilians and as military men and had nothing to show for their labors. "Brother, Can You Spare a Dime?" became a popular song.

Lesson Plan 9

Hoovervilles

OBJECTIVES:

To build a facsimile of a homeless community reminiscent of Hoovervilles, Okievilles, Bonus Army Camps, or Hobo Jungles.

To prepare a Hooverville scene for "A 20th Century America Time Machine."

To compare the salaries of average workers with those of the same workers today.

MATERIALS:

Hooverville construction illustration,* newspaper, packing crates, board appliance boxes in assorted sizes, tarpaper, salvaged materials (flattened cans, boards, shutters); hammers, nails, tape, paint; references: (See Bibliography.) C. Aaron. *Lackawanna*, J. Stanley. *Children of the Dust Bowl,* M. Meltzer. *Brother, Can You Spare a Dime?* ; film or video (see Bibliography); "Average Salaries of Workers in the 1930's."

*Provided at the end of the lesson.

LENGTH OF TIME:

Two 1–hour periods.

PROCEDURE:

1. The teacher asks the students what they could do if their family had no money at all, if their parents were out of work, had used up all their savings, and were unable to pay the mortgage on their home. When students offer suggestions, the teacher in a verbal battle of wits finds a reason why that idea won't work. For example, if the students say the family could move in with the grandparents, the teacher tells them that in this case the grandparents are also having financial difficulty and live in a one–room apartment where there is no room for additional family members. The teacher keeps soliciting suggestions from the students and eliminates them or makes them untenable in some other way until the students finally decide that they might have to live on the streets or in a public park. The teacher then explains that many people during the Great Depression had to do just that. They moved into cardboard villages that became known as Hoovervilles, named after President Hoover. Hoovervilles popped up near cities and communities, in vacant lots, under bridges, and in parks.

2. Using available resources, the teacher shows pictures of these Hoovervilles, people selling apples on the streets, and long soup lines.

3. The teacher reminds the students that the Great Depression occurred before the social welfare programs that we have today and yet even today many people are homeless. Over 35 percent of the men in some parts of the country were without work of any kind. Savings were gone, homes and furniture had been repossessed or sold. Many people were sick and hungry. When they lost their jobs and homes, they turned to makeshift homes made from anything they could find.

4. The teacher further explains that the Bonus Army camps that sprang up added a speaker's platform in the center of the shelters and provided daily news, bulletins, and rousing speeches to the people in these camps. In the dry California lake beds and fields squatter communities sprang up known as Little Oklahomas or Okievilles. The people living in these communities were out of work and hoped to subsist on the remains of crops left from harvests. California growers attempted to get rid of the squatters by burning what remained of their crops.

5. The teacher explains that the students will make a replica of a Hooverville. The class decides how many shelters to build and follow the instructions:

 a. Tape two boxes together to make a larger shelter. The sizes of the buildings should be varied for visual effect. (A)

 b. Cut holes for doors and windows. (B)

 c. Nail on loose boards, any lengths.

 d. Flatten metal containers (#10 food cans and lids, sheet metal pieces) and attach to shelters to cover "holes."

 e. Attach other found building material (tarpaper, shutters).

 f. Optional: Paint advertising on boards and small signs offering services such as "Ironing and washing—5 cents."

 g. Add furniture, clotheslines, pots, kettles, laundry tub, 50–gallon drum (to be used as a stove around which people cook and keep warm).

 h. Set the Hooverville in a hallway, classroom, or exhibit for "A 20th Century America Time Machine."

6. The salaries of those people who did have jobs was quite different from those of today. The students examine the "Average Salaries of Workers in the 1930's," which gives examples of the annual incomes earned by men and women in the early thirties. They then find out the average salary of some of these people today. This research can be done by using the want ads in the newspaper, by interviewing businesses directly, by looking in a current *World Almanac,* or with the help of the reference librarian in the public library.

7. The teacher explains that in order to make a fair comparison between the two times, they will need to know the cost of living. The students locate the average cost of housing, food, and other major items in today's economy. They can compare these two times by expressing them as ratios.

HOOVERVILLE CONSTRUCTION

ALSO FOR OKIEVILLE, BONUS ARMY CAMP, HOBO JUNGLE

Average Salaries of Workers in the 1930's

Coal miner	$723.00	Construction worker	907.00
Dentist	2391.00	Doctor	3382.00
Engineer	2520.00	Fire chief	2075.00
Hired man (farm)	216.00	Lawyer	4218.00
Maid	260.00	Police chief	2636.00
RR Conductor	2729.00	Nurse	936.00
Secretary	1040.00	Steelworker	422.87
Typist	624.00	U.S. Congressman	8663.00
Waitress	520.00	Teacher	1227.00
Bus Driver	1373.00		

Lesson Plan 10
Hobo Hieroglyphs

OBJECTIVES: To understand the communication system developed by hobos as they traveled throughout the country.
To set up a pictorial communication system.

MATERIALS: Worksheet, "Hobo Hieroglyphs;"* chalk or crayons, masking tape, and drawing paper.
*Provided at the end of the lesson.

SPECIAL INSTRUCTIONS: The teacher needs to check with the principal before allowing students to use chalk to draw their hieroglyphs on the walls of the school.

LENGTH OF TIME: 45 minutes.

PROCEDURE:

1. The teacher asks the students what they would do if they were living in a Hooverville but wanted to better themselves. The teacher accepts several varied answers, such as find materials to make it warmer, beg for food, work for a farmer in exchange for food, or travel to other parts of the country to look for work.

2. The teacher tells the students that Hobo jungles or squatter camps were built near railroad tracks and inhabited by transient hobos of all ages who hopped on and off trains. The transients were an odd assortment of people and included fathers looking for work, old men moving on, boys who'd left home and girls who, for protection, dressed as boys. In these camps food, warm fires, and information about train schedules, safe cities, and possible work, were shared. Each new town that they came to might mean a square meal, a warm place to sleep, or even a day's work. Each new town might also be dangerous. Railroad guards could hurt you, or the police could throw you in jail. People who resorted to this life style were usually trying to better their lives. The teacher leads a discussion as to what life as a hobo might have been like by asking questions like the following:

   a. What would you have liked about being a hobo? What would you not have liked?

   b. Do you think that you would have developed a lot of camaraderie?

   c. Where would be the best places to go in your opinion? How would you travel?

   d. How could you let other hobos know about the dangerous or helpful places that you encountered?

3. If the students do not come up with the idea of leaving a secret message for others to find, the teacher tells them that the hobos used picture writing as messages on buildings, fences, doorways, or sidewalks. These messages, called hieroglyphs provided useful information about where to find food, who would offer help, or what places were dangerous. The students are divided into pairs and look at the worksheet, "Hobo

Hieroglyphs." Each pair of students attempts to match the illustrations to the phrases. The teacher asks the entire class for its analysis of which illustration means what. The students must substantiate their reasons.

4. Each pair of students lists five or more other situations that hobos might meet in their travels, such as:

Farmwork help needed here.

Mean lady lives here.

Railroad guards everywhere.

Free meal here.

Bath and clean change of clothes here.

5. The two students create hieroglyphs for each of the situations.

6. The students use chalk to mark their hieroglyphs on the walls and doors of the school. If chalk is unacceptable the students can draw the hieroglyphs with crayon on drawing paper and tape them to the walls and doors.

7. Students from other classes figure out what these hobo hieroglyphs mean.

8. At "A 20th Century America Time Machine" program the parents and others attending are given a definition sheet of signs created by the class and must match the school hobo signs with their correct definitions.

Answers to Hobo Hieroglyphs

1. I

2. A

3. E

4. B

5. G

6. D

7. F

8. C

9. H

Hobo Hieroglyphs

_____ 1.

A. People here will treat you if you're sick.

_____ 2.

B. Trains nearby.

_____ 3.

C. Danger! Man who lives here has a gun!

_____ 4.

D. Handout for hobos.

_____ 5.

E. Bad town. Police watching.

_____ 6.

F. Good doctor/free treatment.

_____ 7.

G. Mean dog!

_____ 8.

H. Handcuffs. You could be jailed!

_____ 9.

I. Nice lady lives here.

Lesson Plan 11

WPA Artists Project

OBJECTIVE: To paint a mural in the style and theme of a WPA Artists Project and display it at "A 20th Century America Time Machine" program or in the Tabletop Museum.

MATERIALS: Fact sheet, "The New Deal";* WPA Artists Project illustrations;* choice of 4' x 8" wallboard, masonite, school hallway wall (permanent display) or 15' sheet of white project roll paper (temporary); outside brick school wall, fencing, rock outcroppings; latex or acrylic paints (for permanent art); tempera paint – 1 quart to 1/2 cup liquid detergent (for temporary art); brushes; J.V. Compton, compiler. Jackdaw, *The New Deal*. (See Bibiliography.)
*Provided at the end of the lesson.

LENGTH OF TIME: Varies.

PROCEDURE:

1. The teacher asks the class if they were President of the United States after the crash, what they would do. All answers are accepted. The students are told that this situation faced the new President, Franklin D. Roosevelt, who was elected for the first time in 1932.

2. The teacher distributes the fact sheet, "The New Deal," and the students read it to find out what happened when Hoover ran for reelection in 1932. Several pictures are shown from the Jackdaw, "The New Deal," (anti–Roosevelt cartoons, the Colt Rower mural detail, the TVA Norris Dam) to show some of the things that did occur. Pictures from other books can be used instead. The teacher leads a discussion on the Roosevelt administration by asking questions like the following:

   a. What conditions existed in the 1930's that President Roosevelt attempted to solve?

   b. What was so new about the New Deal?

   c. Can you see any similarities in the conditions between the 1930's and the 1990's? For example, President Clinton has started the "National Service Program." Find out what this program does and how it is similar to some of Roosevelt's programs.

   d. What social programs were started under President Roosevelt?

   e. Are any of these programs still around today? Should they be?

   f. In your opinion was it a good idea to start these programs?

   g. Can you find evidence of any buildings, bridges, or other projects that were built as a result of the New Deal? (Often the date that appears on bridges over small streams can be easily observed.) How can you find out if your community participated in any of the programs?

g. What event not mentioned in the fact sheet finally put everyone to work?

3. **The teacher helps the students to organize and plan a mural showing themselves as part of a program to benefit their own community. Suggestions are planting trees, removing debris and brush to make a playground or park, or clearing a vacant lot for a baseball field.**

4. **The students draw preliminary sketches and incorporate their individual ideas. The mural is finished by completing the instructions:**

a. **Transfer drawings onto the large working area you've chosen. Draw large, so that there is little background to fill in. (A)**

A

b. **Try to have as much dark color as light color to obtain good contrast. (B)**

B

c. **After mural is painted, put in detail (texture) such as printed shirts, hair, stitching on jeans. The more detail, the better the mural. Outline everything in black. (C)**

WPA

ARTISTS PROJECT

C

The New Deal

Where was America going? Could this downhill trend be slowed? America didn't have to think twice about voting in a new president. Franklin Delano Roosevelt assumed office on March 4, 1933. The previous year had been the most devastating depression year of all. People turned to him for relief and salvation. What could he do to turn the country around, promote work, help the elderly, homeless, and the destitute? In a speech during his campaign he said, "It makes sense to try an idea. If it does not work, admit it frankly and try another. But above all, try something." In his Inaugural Address he said, "Our greatest primary task is to put people to work."

Through a series of "fireside chats" broadcast on the radio Roosevelt talked to the forgotten people of America. To work was a right not a privilege. He was on their side, and they would be taken care of. No longer would they fall through the cracks. He proposed a New Deal—a series of new programs aimed to relieve, improve, rehabilitate and reform the nation's problems. To do these things he developed public–works projects and initiated the Federal Emergency Relief Administration (FERA) that acted as a bandaid but gave money to the needy to tide them over. Many refused this relief money as they didn't want to be on the dole.

The Works Progress Administration (WPA) had only a 5–year life span. Though it gave jobs to four million people some likened the program as "something–to–do" work with little practical value. To them the initials might have meant "We peel apples." The WPA, however, initiated the building of bridges, buildings, parks, schools, and roads, and established arts programs for unemployed artists and musicians (called the Federal Arts Project, Federal Writers Project and Federal Theater Project). These artists documented local life through murals and organized community theaters. Many of these public improvements are still being used today.

Roosevelt also provided work for young people. His National Youth Administration (NYA) gave part–time jobs, loans, and education to students. His Civilian Conservation Corps (CCC) was very successful. Two and a half million young people were trained in skills and worked on conservation projects such as fish restocking in streams and ponds, planting trees, and fighting forest fires. They planted over two million trees, fought Dutch Elm disease, dug drainage ditches, and built campgrounds. They lived in camps, received room and board, had medical care, and earned a salary, part of which they were required to send home to their families. The Public Works Admininistration (PWA) instituted construction jobs on hospitals, city halls, sewage disposal plants, bridges and educational buildings.

Roosevelt's National Recovery Act (NRA) was controversial. This program was a regulator of competition, prices, production, wages and working hours through a system of codes. Its logo—the blue eagle—with the slogan, "We do our part," was a familiar New Deal sight. The NRA came under much criticism because people felt it had too

many codes and not enough supervision. Big business had more clout. The NRA was declared unconstitutional by the U.S. Supreme Court.

The New Deal provided for employment for the jobless, supported crop prices, repealed Prohibition, stopped home foreclosures, ensured bank deposits, stabilized the economy, and initiated social security and unemployment insurance. It wasn't the whole answer, but it greatly helped the American people at that time.

APPLE SELLERS

Lesson Plan 12

Civilian Conservation Corps (CCC)

Community Beautification

OBJECTIVE: To decide on and plan a conservation activity in your community.

MATERIALS: Varies depending upon project initiated; "Foyer Flora" illustration as an example; "Decision–Making Process Sheet" (similar to that provided in Lesson Plan 11 in the *For Better* section of this book.)

SPECIAL INSTRUCTIONS: The students need to include certain things within their criteria such as approval of the principal or other authority, methods of meeting any cost or donations, when to do the work, how to enlist adult help for their expertise, supervision, and errand–running.

LENGTH OF TIME: Varies, depending on project.

PROCEDURE:

1. The teacher explains that President Roosevelt felt a strong need to get young people involved in making this country a better place. He established the Civilian Conservation Corps, which provided temporary jobs for young people in forest conservation. The teacher and students discuss what might be a good beautification or conservation project for the school or neighborhood. They examine the illustration of the example project, "Foyer Flora."

2. In order to select a project, the teacher and students set five or more criteria for making a decision about a conservation activity that would be vital for community improvement or beautification that they might be able to carry out. They use a "Decision–Making Process Sheet" similar to that in Lesson 11 of the *For Better* section of this book and record their criteria.

3. The class brainstorms activities that could be tried. All ideas are accepted at this point. The criteria are applied later. Examples might include:

- Clear vacant lot for playground, community garden.
- Clean up an existing park; plant perennials, trees or shrubs.
- Plant a flower and/or vegetable garden on school property.
- Build an indoor garden in school lobby.

4. A grid is set up for making the decision similar to that used in Lesson 11 of the *For Better* section of this book. The criteria are listed down the left side of the grid, and the ideas are listed across the top of the grid. Groups of two students rank each of the ideas. The groups report to the entire class, and consensus is reached about the best idea.

5. The class states their objective and draws a sketch of what the project will look like when completed.

6. The class lists all the materials they will need and how they will get them.

7. The class lists any problems they believe they may encounter in completing the activity and how they will solve that problem.

8. The class implements the plan.

FOYER FLORA

Lesson Plan 13

Dust Bowl Corn

OBJECTIVE: To simulate the devastation of losing corn crops by planting corn and watching it wither from lack of water.

MATERIALS: Potting soil or moistened vermiculite and liquid fertilizer, 4–5 window boxes or 8–10 large flower pots, seed corn; J. Stanley. *Children of the Dust Bowl* (see Bibliography).

SPECIAL INSTRUCTIONS: Children often plant seed as part of science projects. This activity is intended to teach them about loss and hardship experienced by farmers living in the midwest in the thirties. In this activity, it is important that each student becomes attached to his/her seedling. The teacher soaks the seed corn overnight in water the night before it is to be planted. If vermiculite is used, the seedlings must receive liquid fertilizer as vermiculite provides no nutrition.

LENGTH OF TIME: Approximately 10 days for germination, less if seed is soaked; 3 weeks for growth.

PROCEDURE:

1. The teacher shows the class photos from *Children of the Dust Bowl* and reads excerpts from the book that describe conditions and hardships that families in the midwest had to endure before pulling up stakes and leaving their homes and farms. The students discuss the hardships of farmers living in the Dust Bowl during the 1930's. They describe how these farmers must have felt when their crops began to wither from lack of water.

2. Students review the needs of growing plants and prepare the soil for planting. Window boxes or flower pots can be arranged in a row along the windows in the classroom.

3. Each student is given a kernel of corn to plant. The corn kernel is carefully pushed down into the soil. No more than six kernels are planted per window box, one or two in each flower pot. The location where the seed is planted is marked with a sign attached to a toothpick or popsicle stick. Names are given to each of the seeds and written on the location signs.

4. Each student writes in a diary on a daily basis of the corn seed he or she has planted. They should include thoughts they have, ideas about their plant names, anything they do to enhance the environment around the plant, and similar things. They are to tend their plants faithfully, creating a home for each plant. For example, students are encouraged to create stick fences around their plants or tiny stone walls. They can place small plastic animals like a deer or dog near the plant. The more familiar and protective the students are of their plants the more effective the activity will be.

5. The soil in the window boxes or flower pots is kept moist but not wet.

6. Seeds germinate in about 10 days or less if they have been soaked overnight before planting. Students may wish to water their own seedlings, or members of the class may take turns. The seedlings are watered for 3 weeks. (If vermiculite is used, liquid fertilizer is mixed with the water.) It is best to water lightly every day. Students should remember, however, to check the soil as too much water can harm the plants. If some seeds have not germinated after ten days, additional seeds can be planted.

7. The teacher asks students to check their seedlings daily.

8. At the end of three weeks the students are told to discontinue watering as a drought has come to the land. They are to watch the plants carefully to see what effect this drought will have on their plants. They continue to care for and write about their plants.

9. As the plants begin to wither, the students record their feelings and reactions in their diaries. The teacher should be prepared for some students watering their plants in secret or insisting upon it. If this watering occurs, the student must write about it in his or her diary including all reasons why it was done.

10. As the plants deteriorate further, the students are asked to include in their diaries how they will fell when the plant dies and what it must have been like for the farmers and their families to see whole fields of corn and wheat wither and die in the heat and dust.

11. A successful activity is one in which students have internalized a situation. If this has happened, and the class expresses a wish to do so, resume watering the plants.

Bibliography

1920–1930

Allen, Frederick Lewis. *Only Yesterday: An Informal History of the 1920s.* New York: Harper & Row, 1984.

Originally published in 1931, this book tells of the 1920's from the collapse of Wilson to the stock market crash. Absorbing but sometimes hard to wade through.

Hobbler, Dorothy & Thomas. *And Now, A Word From Our Sponsor: The Story of a Roaring Twenties Girl.* Englewood Cliffs, NJ: Silver Burdett Press, 1992.

Charming fictional account about a young girl who builds her own crystal radio and ultimately has an airplane ride with Charles Lindbergh.

Klingaman, William K. *1929: The Year of the Great Crash.* New York: Harper & Row, 1989.

Using first–person accounts, Dr. Klingaman gives us a better understanding of the art, sports, economics, and politics of this period.

TIME–LIFE. *This Fabulous Century 1920–1930.* Alexandria, VA: Time–Life Books, 1969.

Covers the Roaring 20's, barnstorming, radio, jazz age, prohibition, and much more.

Perrett, Geoffrey. *America In The Twenties: A History.* New York: Simon & Schuster, 1982.

This book shows strong similarities and contrasts of the twenties to our own era. Gives an excellent look at the people of that period and exposes the sharp contrasts created by mixing new and old ideas and customs.

Pinkney, Gloria Jean. *Back Home.* New York: Dial Books for Young Readers, 1992.

Wonderful illustrations by Jerry Pinkney, this book gives the story of a young child who visits relatives on a North Carolina farm.

Wallner, Alexandra. *Since 1920.* New York: A Doubleday Book for Young Readers; Delacourte Press, 1992.

Picture book depicting a neighborhood and its growth from 1920.

Films

Bugsy Malone (1976). Video available. Rated PG.

A spoof on gangster movies.

Dinner at Eight (1933). Video available. No rating provided. (Jean Harlow, John Barrymore, Wallace Beery, Marie Dressler).

This movie is about a dinner party so that a lot of typical conversation of the twenties occurs.

Mrs. Parker and the Vicious Circle (1994). No video available. (Jennifer Jason Leigh and Campbell Scott).

This film shows the wicked wit of the Round Table but is not widely available. It was shown at the 1994 Boston Film Festival.

Swing High, Swing Low (1937). Video available. No rating provided. (Carole Lombard and Fred MacMurray).

Shows the world of the jazz musician.

The Little Rascals (1994). No video available. No rating available.

Based on the *Our Gang* short films of 1922–1944, this film shows the clothing of the time.

Top Hat (1935). Video available. No rating provided. (Fred Astaire and Ginger Rogers).

Gives an overview for the decade.

1930–1940

Aaron, Chester. *Lackawanna*. New York: J.B. Lippincott, 1986.

Historical fiction about a group of ragtag kids riding the rails during the Depression.

Allen, Frederick Lewis. *Since Yesterday: The 1930's in America*. New York: Harper & Row, 1986.

An excellent look of the 1930's and what happened as the result of the stock market crash.

Bronin, Andrew. Jackdaw No. A11. *The Depression*. Box A03, Amawalk, NY: Jackdaw Pub. Ltd., 1972, reprinted 1990.

Primary resource material includes pictures from a family album; depression script; newspaper headlines; campaign flyers and auction sale posters.

Compton, James V, compiler. *The New Deal . Amawalk, NY, Golden Owl Publishing Co., 1990.*

This Jackdaw contains primary resource material (facsimiles of front–page news on Roosevelt's fireside chats; social security message; leaflets for a UAW protest meeting; and cartoons.

Hamilton, Virginia. *Drylongso*. New York: Harcourt Brace Jovanovich, 1992.

Jerry Pinkney's Drylongso appears at a family's farm during a terrible dust storm. The story of a family living west of the Mississippi River. Although the story takes place in the 1970's it is very typical of conditions during the difficult 1930's.

Meltzer, Milton. *Brother, Can You Spare a Dime? — The Great Depression 1929–1933*. New York: Penguin Books, 1969.

Meltzer doesn't let us down with this provocative book. Excellent coverage of a tragic time in our history, the causes and consequences and a look at the people who were affected by the depression.

Pendergraft, Patricia. *As Far As Mill Springs*. New York: Philomel Books, 1991.

During the depression 12 year–old Robert runs away from an awful foster home to find his mother. His friend, Abiah, and a mutt dog ride the rails with him.

Seeger, Pete and Reiser, Bob. *Carry It On*. Bethlehem, PA: Sing Out Publication, 1991.

A collection of songs about working people from the eighteenth century on.

Stanley, Jerry. *Children of the Dust Bowl: The True Story of the School at Weedpatch Camp*. New York: Crown Publishers, Inc. 1992.

Tells about the problems of migrant workers who traveled from the Dust Bowl to find work in California only to find descrimination and ridicule. These Oklahoman children (called "dumb Oakies"), together with a sympathetic Superintendent of Schools, built their own school.

Steinbeck, John. *In Dubious Battle*. New York: Penguin Books, 1986.

Tells a tale of an uprising of migrant workers against landowners in California apple country. It is the eternal human fight against injustice.

Taylor, Mildred D. *Song of the Trees*. New York: Bantam Books, 1975.

Based on a true story, this book tells of a southern black family who try to protect their woodlot from unscrupulous loggers until their father, away looking for work, comes home.

Terkel, Studs. *Hard Times: An Oral History of The Great Depression*. New York: Pantheon Books, 1970.

Interviews of 75 people throughout America during 1930's — the destitute and the very wealthy, some famous, many living in quiet and not so quiet desperation, and all affected by the Depression.

TIME–LIFE. *This Fabulous Century 1930–1940*. Alexandria, VA: Time–Life Books, 1969.

Covers New Deal, Hoovervilles, jive talk, annual earnings and more.

Films

The Eleanor Roosevelt Story (1965). No video available. No rating provided.

Black and white biographical documentary.

The Great Gatsby (1974). Video available. Rated PG. (Robert Redford and Mia Farrow).

Covers the subjects of prohibition and the Jazz Age quite well. Earlier version also available. Based on book by F. Scott Fitzgerald.

The Journey of Natty Gann (1985). Video available. Rated PG. (Meredith Salenger).

In this high quality Walt Disney film, Natty travels across the U.S. during the Great Depression to search for her father.